Gemini

22 May – 21 June

First published in Great Britain 2010
by Harlequin Mills & Boon Limited,
Eton House, 18-24 Paradise Road, Richmond, Surrey TW9 1SR

Copyright © Dadhichi Toth 2007, 2008, 2009, 2010 & 2011

ISBN: 978 0 263 87380 1

Typeset at Midland Typesetters Australia

Harlequin Mills & Boon policy is to use papers that are
natural, renewable and recyclable products and made from
wood grown in sustainable forests. The logging and
manufacturing processes conform to the legal environmental
regulations of the country of origin.

Printed and bound in Spain
by Litografia Rosés S.A., Barcelona

About
Dadhichi

Dadhichi is one of Australia's foremost astrologers. He has the ability to draw from complex astrological theory to provide clear, easily understandable advice and insights for people who want to know what their future might hold.

In the 27 years that Dadhichi has been practising astrology, face reading and other esoteric studies, he has conducted over 9,500 consultations. His clients include celebrities, political and diplomatic figures, and media and corporate identities from all over the world.

Dadhichi's unique blend of astrology and face reading helps people fulfil their true potential. His extensive experience practising western astrology is complemented by his research into the theory and practice of eastern systems of astrology.

Dadhichi features in numerous newspapers and magazines and he also appears regularly on many of Australia's leading television and radio networks, where many of his political and world-wide forecasts have proved uncannily accurate.

His website www.astrology.com.au is now one of the top ten online Australian lifestyle sites and, in conjunction with www.facereader.com, www. soulconnector.com and www.psychjuice.com, they attract over half a million visitors monthly. The websites offer a wide variety of features, helpful information and personal services.

Dedicated to The Light of Intuition
Sri V. Krishnaswamy—mentor and friend
With thanks to Julie, Joram, Isaac and Janelle

Welcome from
Dadhichi

Dear Friend,

Welcome to your astrological forecast for 2011! I've spent considerable time preparing these insights for you. My goal is to give you an overview of your sign and I hope you can use my simple suggestions to steer you in the right direction.

I am often asked by my clients to help them understand their true path and what they are supposed to be doing in life. This is a complex task; however, astrology can assist with finding some answers. In this book I attempt to reveal those unique character traits that define who you are. With a greater self-understanding, you can effectively begin to *live who you are* rather than wondering about *what you should do*. Identity is the key!

Knowing when the best opportunities in your life are likely to appear is the other benefit of astrology, based on planetary transits and forecasting. The latter part of the book deals with what is *likely* to happen on a yearly, monthly and daily basis. By coupling this section with the last chapter, an effective planner, you can conduct your business, relationships and personal affairs in ways that yield maximum benefits for you.

Along with your self-knowledge, there are two other key attributes you must carry with you: *trust* and *courage*. Unless you're prepared to take a gamble in life, earnestly and fearlessly, you'll stay stuck in the same place, never really growing or progressing. At some point you have to take a step forward. When you synchronise yourself with the powerful talents found in your Sun sign, you'll begin to understand what your mission in life will be. This is the true purpose and use of astrology.

So I invite you to gear up for an exciting fifteen months! Don't shrink back from life, even if at times some of the forecasts seem a little daunting. Don't forget that humans are always at their best when the going gets tough. The difficult planetary transits are merely invitations to bring out the best in yourself, while the favourable planetary cycles are seasons for enjoying the benefits that karma has in store for you.

Remain positive, expect the best, and see the beauty in everyone and everything. Remember the words of a great teacher: 'The world is as you see it.' In other words, life will reflect back to you only what you are willing to see.

I trust the coming fifteen months will grant you wonderful success, health, love and happiness. May the light of the Sun, the Moon and all of the stars fill your heart with joy and satisfaction.

Your Astrologer,

Dadhichi Toth

Contents

The Gemini
Identity

Any idiot can face a crisis. It's day-to-day living that wears you out.

—Anton Chekhov

Gemini: A Snapshot

Key Characteristics

Versatile, intellectual, communicative, social, scattered, inquisitive, loves variety and change

Compatible Star Signs

Leo, Libra, Sagittarius, Aquarius and Aries

Key Life Phrase

I think

Life Goals

To be respected for your intelligence; to be creative, original and fun to be around

Platinum Assets

Lightning-quick reflexes, multi-tasker, inspirational and fun

Zodiac Totem

The Twins

Zodiac Symbol

Ⅱ

Zodiac Facts

Third sign of the zodiac; mutable, masculine and positive, barren

Element

Air

Famous Geminis

Meryl Streep, Anna Kournikova, Tim Allen, Mike Myers, Venus Williams, Jamie Oliver, Kylie Minogue, Lenny Kravitz, John F. Kennedy, Brooke Shields, Steve Waugh, Stevie Nicks, Gladys Knight, Sir Paul McCartney, Johnny Depp, Angelina Jolie, Colin Farrell, Ice Cube, Bob Dylan, Errol Flynn, Priscilla Presley

Gemini: Your profile

I don't think I've ever met a boring Gemini. It's true that if you're born under Gemini you do have the tendency to talk a lot. But even so, for the most part I've found people under your star sign always have something extremely interesting to say and quite often are highly intelligent.

Mercury is your ruling planet, which gives you your trademark communication skills *par excellence*, which others admire and respect in you. This planet also gives you incredibly quick wit, original ideas and an inventive personality. Creativity of a high order is evident in people born under the sign of the twins.

Communicating ideas—linking your mind with others and developing new and unusual systems of thought—is what you are primarily interested in. One thing everyone notices about you is the fact that you're always busy, never stopping to take a breath, and at the same time quite inexhaustible in your source of energy. 'Where do you get your stamina?' people ask.

Well, that stamina may sometimes be short lived. You are in fact a person who gives 110 per cent to everything you do, but as a result, you also have the tendency to run yourself ragged. You need to manage your physical and mental energies a little more carefully to optimise your sense of wellbeing. You mustn't burn the candle at both ends.

You are the type of person who's curious about life and therefore loves to learn about anything and everything. You have a broad base of knowledge. Consequently you can sometimes be accused of being a little superficial because you like to taste a bit of this and a bit of that, very much like a connoisseur of food at a smorgasbord. But yet again, you have such a diverse range of interests that you're happy to forego the 'main course' for the excitement of a wider experience. Gemini is constantly on the prowl for stimulation and education.

Restlessness is one of your less-positive traits, but here again we see that this is what gives you the drive to seek new adventures in life and to keep learning more and more. For you, the idea of growing old is abhorrent. In fact, your ruling planet Mercury is youthful even in old age, imbuing you with this quality. Many of the same Geminis I referred to earlier seem to appear much younger than their age, both physically and in the way they communicate their experiences. 'Growing old gracefully' is not in your repertoire.

Gemini is a dual sign, which means you're the butt of many 'schizophrenic' jokes. This does have some truth to it, especially when we delve more deeply into the Gemini character to see that you do blow hot and cold from time to time. On the one hand, you want something; on the other hand, you don't. Sometimes you want more; sometimes you want less, and so on. A see-saw of expectations does present you with challenges surrounding who you are and what your true identity is. Try not to allow others to misinterpret this as some sort of deliberately deceptive personality flaw on your part, because it's not.

Getting down to a routine is not something you enjoy all that much. Rather, you'd prefer an intense array of variety to keep you on the edge, even if it does affect your nervous system sometimes. Words, poetry, even music or other forms of verbal communication, are your forte. Taking an interest in writing or teaching—even if they aren't things you might consider doing professionally—are right up your alley.

Because of your insatiable desire to learn and communicate, you have an extraordinarily wide circle of friends and interests. In fact, you may have several different groups of friends to satisfy your never-ending search for understanding. Try not to spread yourself too thinly, however, because you'll make commitments in good faith only to find that you have run out of time and aren't capable of giving equally to those you love.

You are a traveller by nature and the restlessness of spirit that is part and parcel of your character will have you journeying to many different parts of the world to explore culture, history and anthropology. Even if you don't travel overseas, you will find yourself constantly moving, travelling or even just walking to burn off some of that nervous energy.

Three classes of Gemini

Being born between the 22nd of May and the 1st of June makes you a Gemini with a cusp influence of the previous sign, Taurus. Although you're primarily an intellectual type with intense Mercurial influences, Venus, the ruler of Taurus, also imprints upon you considerable sensuality, grace and charm. You not only love the written word, intellectual pursuits and other forms of communication, but may gravitate towards artistic, musical and creative activities to express your inner need for cultural perfection.

If you're a Gemini born between the 2nd and the 12th of June, you also have a tendency to be sensual but have the influence of Libra as well, which makes you at times indecisive about your life path. You need clarity in your choice of partners and must never impulsively rush into any sort of relationship.

If you're born between the 13th and the 21st of June, the influence of Aquarius and the unpredictable planet Uranus has a sway over your life and your temperament. You are spontaneous in many areas of your existence and like to explore the unknown. Your life will swing from the positive to the negative so you must be prepared for some turbulent times on your journey. At least you'll never be bored with the challenges that are presented to you. As you grow older and develop more wisdom, you're likely to be regarded as someone with extraordinary knowledge and a capacity to help those around you. Your path is one of compassion and humanitarianism.

Gemini role model: Mike Myers

If you've ever seen Mike Myers, the famous Hollywood comedian and actor, you'll gain a clear insight into the Gemini personality. Full of fun, clever one-liners and an intensely creative nature generally, Mike symbolises the true Gemini spirit. Just like him, you have an immense amount of potential talent, which should be used in a clear and focused manner for the best results.

Gemini: The light side

If you meet an unintelligent Gemini, let me assure you it's probably because they're pretending to play the sucker to catch a sucker, and that's you! The Gemini mind is quick, agile and full of dazzling brilliance. You'll need lightning-fast reflexes to keep up with their abilities.

Geminis are able to lighten other people's loads. When times are tough and people feel dark, sombre and overwhelmed by life's challenges, Geminis have the wonderful ability to use humour to make people feel that life's not all as bad as it appears to be. You know, this is one of their greatest gifts.

Networking is one of your key abilities, Gemini. Both socially and professionally, you know how to make friends and persuade them to come along with you for the Gemini ride. You make an excellent salesperson, public relations expert, or generally just a great storyteller because your words are well chosen to captivate others.

You're unbiased in your opinion because you're able to see everyone's perspective and don't necessarily take sides. However, if you do feel strongly enough in your convictions, it's pretty hard to beat you in an argument. You take pleasure in letting others know you are right.

In life, your flexibility will be a major asset in allowing you to achieve success by being able to 'shift gears midway' when changes are necessary.

Gemini: The shadow side

It's often hard for you to be completely honest with others, and not at all because you're trying to deceive them. There are so many different layers to your personality that perhaps, at least in the first part of your life, you're not quite sure of your identity and which of the many personalities within you is the real you!

This journey of self-discovery must be conducted in a way that doesn't transmit the wrong signals to others. This may be difficult because you are such a changeable character, exhibiting so many dazzling aspects of your nature, very much like a multi-faceted diamond. But some people are not able to understand you and therefore this could get them offside.

Speak slowly and clearly when you are communicating, especially if the message is of paramount importance. Your speed sometimes causes people to feel that you're going over their heads, looking down at them and giving them the impression that you are mentally arrogant.

In your social endeavours, try to sit back and listen a little. You can learn a lot by hearing what others have to say, which also takes the pressure off you having to be the keynote speaker in every circumstance. Listen as much as you speak.

Gemini woman

As a female born under the sign of Gemini, your primary element of air indicates, like air itself, that you are very difficult to constrain or understand. Being able to describe the Gemini female personality precisely requires considerable mental dexterity. Air moves and flows in a free sort of manner.

Some women born under Gemini are definitely 'air heads'; they are scattered, like a shotgun, blasting its way in all directions simultaneously. But that's not the case with all of you. The more refined Gemini lass has the ability to take control of these many different psychological and emotional energies and focus them to her distinct advantage.

Once you do gain control of your inner life, your Mercurial humour and charm will win the hearts of many. That natural flair for words and your genuine interest in human nature will make you loved by one and all. Your equal ability to stimulate an individual or a group makes you sought after in any social situation.

Creativity flows through your veins. You need to create to feel alive. This may not necessarily appear through painting, music or other such accepted conventions, but could at least appear in the way you express yourself in your relationships. People will soon see that you are original and independent. Such versatile actresses as Annette Benning and Angelina Jolie, as well as the famous comedian Joan Rivers, are all born under your Gemini birth sign and share the brilliance of Mercury with you.

Gemini women move quickly. If you blink, they can disappear in a moment. For those wanting to engage in social or romantic connections with you, they need to be quick off the mark. There's a certain level of impatience in the way you live your life, as if time is of the essence and you don't want to miss one moment of this glorious adventure.

Those Gemini women born on the cusp, as mentioned earlier in the identity readings, have a flair for fashion, and are able to make a statement with the way they dress and present themselves.

You may not be quite as flashy in the way you use words, but your use of colour will hit the mark when and where you need it most.

Gemini females born in the middle of the month make great negotiators and mediators. You'll be a valued friend to your group because you always know how to make fair judgements and advise others along the same lines.

The wackier Geminis who love spontaneity and are in a sense rebels without a cause, are born in the last one-third of the month. As you can see, there are many different grades and flavours to the female Gemini personality, each as interesting and exciting as the others.

Other women will envy you in a way because you're able to maintain the youthful quality of your physical being thanks to Mercury having its major rulership over your star sign. Your skin seems to maintain its elasticity and, along with your bright and vivacious mind, people will often note that you look and act so much younger than your actual age. Between you and me, I'm happy to keep your age a secret. Milk it for all it's worth, Gemini!

Your imagination is a powerful thing and because you are well endowed with it you are sure to be successful in life, irrespective of the path that you choose. You need to negotiate with others but don't rely overly on your physical attractiveness to woo people, especially in the professional arena. You have enough intellectual credentials to compete and play people at their game on their own terms and still come out a winner.

Gemini man

Gemini men are no less intellectually gifted than their female counterparts, with the exception that they may be a little pushier in the way they present their opinions.

As a man born under the star sign of Gemini, your greatest strength is in your mental powers. Communicating your ideas and getting your point across are important to you, but the desire to be right often clouds your judgement. Being right is not always the best way to win a friend or make an ally. Remember that.

The Gemini male is a restless soul, sometimes not quite settling into himself until the second part of his life. This is actually a good thing, mainly because unless and until you've experienced and explored the world enough, you may never truly know what it is you love to do most and why you want to do it. It will only be through exposing yourself to many new experiences and people that you will finally decide on your path when it suits you.

Far from using arguments or scathing sarcasm, which is also one of the most effective tools of a Gemini male, diplomacy is probably a better choice as a way to beat your opponent or win over a friend.

Basically what I'm trying to say is that you need to relax a little, and not push too hard to get others to appreciate you. You have enough redeeming qualities in your personality to gain people's respect without embellishment.

It's not easy to tie down the Gemini man, and I'm not just talking about potential partners. Even your male friends will find you chameleon-like and a little 'slippery', like Mercury. This is because you're just so busy in life and often don't have enough time to share more of it with friends. What am I talking about: you rarely have time for yourself! Always on the go, with a new project in mind, someone to see, someone to help, a new job interview to go to, and so on. Life is like that for the Gemini male.

Your innovative nature seeks out originality. You want to be different to others and create something that makes you stand out from the rest. In due course, you will achieve something that is uniquely you; but when it comes to making commitments, your restlessness makes it difficult for you to give your heart to someone exclusively.

You are eclectic by nature, which means you like diversity in your interests as well as a diversity of friends in your life.

It may serve you well simply to find a couple of friends and deepen your understanding with them. Savour your relationships; no, actually, savour each and every moment. The next moment is not always a greener pasture to chase after because, if you do, you could miss the beauty and the pleasure of the present moment. Try not to scatter your energies too far and wide and life will become a much more enjoyable adventure.

Gemini child

The child of Gemini is certainly cute enough, but ever so fidgety! These children are most definitely some of the most restless of the zodiac signs and they will test your patience, no end.

Also being strong, physically fit, mentally quick and generally fast yourself will be distinct advantages when you are rearing this bundle of energy.

What you'll notice immediately with the Gemini child is that they have an incredibly warm sense of humour. But, if this is taken to extremes, they could end up being the joker, playing pranks and maybe even lashing out with jokes at the expense of others.

There is a cheeky side to their nature and, if you're the parent of a Gemini child, you're already fully aware of this without me having to reiterate it here. The secret of raising a well-integrated Gemini child is communication. You need to engage them intellectually and talk to them about their feelings and their thoughts.

Just as important is to keep your child not only busily occupied with tasks, projects and other hobbies and sporting activities, but in particular to teach them the value of completing what they begin.

Gemini children have a tendency to scatter their energies in many different directions, which makes it difficult for them to set a goal and achieve it. By disciplining them early and also showing them the value of self-discipline, too, you'll be able to overcome these slight character flaws.

Diet is also very important to keep in mind when raising your Gemini child. These kids are prone to skipping meals and living on their nerves. Over time, this can produce behavioural problems if it isn't checked. Pay special attention to their food combinations and also the environment and times of the day in which they eat. All of these factors will have an immense impact on their moods and concentration levels.

As they grow older you'll need to monitor them. This is a critical time in their development when they may overstep the bounds of their mental and physical endurance and may not handle it all that well. Be a friend as well as a good counsellor to them, for this will help them grow into well-adjusted adults.

Romance, love and marriage

The basis of any successful relationship is open, honest communication and fortunately for you, Gemini, this is one of your most accessible and in-built personality traits. This means it's only natural for you to want to communicate your ideas and feelings to the one you love.

Gemini is an air sign, which rules the mental

aspects of human nature and, although you do communicate well, you may have the tendency at times to let your head overrule your heart. You tend to filter your feelings through your mind. Be aware of the need to be more in touch with your instinctive feelings if you are to take your relationships to the next level.

Although you never have a problem connecting with people generally and making lots of friends and new acquaintances, the idea of commitment does tend to scare you a little. You have a desire to be free and independent. As long as your partner can afford you the space to grow as an individual then maybe, just maybe, the big 'C' word won't terrify you too much.

You have an incredibly versatile personality and you love variety. Sticking to one relationship might be difficult for this reason as well. You love the experience of exploring the world, meeting people and trying different things. You see this as a way of expanding your mind and would love your partner to view life in the same way.

Sometimes, however, in a marriage or committed relationship, you could find that it's not always as easy to do this once the day-to-day grind sets in and your family responsibilities take over. It would take a very special type of person to give you the freedom to continue along this sort of lifestyle, and you hope that, when the right person does come along, they too have a similar desire to live a free and exciting life with you.

True love to you means being free enough to express yourself on all levels—intellectually, physically and emotionally. Because your mind is such a dominant part of your being, it's quite likely that creative visualisation and fantasising will play prominent roles in your love life. Sharing your sensual and sexual fantasies with another requires a high degree of trust, wouldn't you agree?

Ideally your soulmate will understand and encourage your diverse interests and your sometimes rather unbelievable ambitions. For you, a marriage partner needs to connect with your ideals as well as aspire to support you in attaining these extraordinary life goals.

There are times when your Gemini mind just can't help being cynical and this is one aspect of your personality that needs to be checked when, and if, you embark on your love life. Unleashing your critical side is never meant to cause hurt, although at times touches of sarcasm will be thrown in to your comments to make your point. Usually, however, you have the other person's best interests at heart and genuinely want to help them grow and become happy and fulfilled within themselves. However, you need to understand that not everyone is as intellectual as you are. Once again, please bear in mind that relating to others on a feeling level rather than a mental or intellectual platform is often a superior way to help them, after all.

You do tend to impose your opinions on others and, in the extreme, they can perceive you as an

opinionated and even self-righteous type of character. You find this amusing but remember, being in
a committed relationship is a long-term thing, and
so this kind of attitude may not be tolerated by the
one whom you consider your soulmate. Try listening
to people a little more to get to know how they are
reacting to what you have to say.

When all is said and done you are a loyal,
passionate and exciting person to be with, and
the energy you bring to a relationship is formidable. Once you consider someone worthy of
your love, you sacrifice a great deal for them, but
the question is usually one of endurance with a
Gemini. As long as your partner can satisfy your
desire for variety and novelty, you will be able to
make the commitment and hang in there for the
long haul.

Health, wellbeing and diet

If you are a typical Gemini you generally don't put
on too much weight and in fact find it quite easy to
burn off calories due to your high metabolic rate.
Other star signs probably envy you for this reason.
If you're a typical Gemini, you're probably a little
leaner than the rest of your zodiac cousins, so this
in itself is a great indicator of health and overall
vitality.

Leaning on your nerves, you risk burnout and
many Geminis I have come in contact with do at
times suffer from nervous exhaustion and other
nerve- or stress-related issues.

Take time for the simple things in life, including sleep and a slower pace generally. Restore some balance to your frazzled nerves and don't make your mealtimes a race to the finish line.

The Gemini, being an air sign, is affected by the lungs, bronchial tubes, shoulders, arms and hands, so you must pay careful attention to your breathing so that your oxygen intake is adequate and can supply sufficient blood to these organs. It's not a good idea for Geminis to smoke because you also have the natural constitutional weakness that can lead to bronchitis, asthma and other pulmonary problems.

On a dietary level, certain foods produce digestive complications and this can result in flatulence and other disturbances. Don't mix your food types and take notes on how even the most ordinary diet affects your body. It's better to learn from your own experiences than from books.

Don't overdo sport because moderate exercise is better for you. Light walking, tennis, swimming and yoga are ideal.

Lean, high-protein foods are also a wonderful way for you to increase your level of energy. Oats and other all-grains such as muesli are the perfect start to the day. Make sure you eat breakfast each morning.

Work

Geminis are the thinkers of the zodiac and therefore

it's not surprising to find them in many organi-sations coming up with ideas, communicating, handling public relations and other such people-orientated activities.

You have an immensely creative mind but also like to be out and about. A balance between working at your desk and exploring in the field would be perfect for a mind such as yours.

Quite a few Gemini-born natives enjoy entre-preneurial work and can run their own businesses because they are naturally gifted at sales and marketing. You'll shine in these particular spheres. I've also seen many Geminis possessing excep-tional skills with their hands. Woodworkers, musicians, jewellers and those who need to do fine-detailed work with their hands are often born under Gemini.

You have tremendous initiative and also the ability to inspire and work with others. You have high expectations because your standards are very precise and others often struggle to meet your demands. You need to teach by example and become a little more sensitive to the needs of your co-workers and those who work around you. As an employee, however, you may sometimes outshine your master.

Jobs such as teaching, lecturing, writing, acting and also the travel-related industries seem to be natural fits if you're born under the sign of Gemini.

Key to karma, spirituality and emotional balance

On karmic and spiritual levels, Aquarius has a strong influence on those born under Gemini. Developing your higher mind, controlling and directing your thought processes and not allowing the trivial issues of life impact on you are all part of the natural, spiritual movement towards self-development and personal evolution.

Your key words are 'I think'. But remember, 'I think' does not mean to over think. Focus on what you're doing and don't let your mind become your master. Rather, it should be your slave. Learning to balance thought with emotion is your challenge.

You like to live in an intense environment, so creating harmony through meditation on a daily basis will be a perfect antidote to your highly strung nature. With this sort of discipline, you'll achieve a great deal of satisfaction and your future karma will be much more fulfilling.

Your lucky days

Your luckiest days are Wednesdays, Fridays and Saturdays.

Your lucky numbers

Remember that the forecasts given later in the book will help you optimise your chances of winning. Your lucky numbers are:

5, 14, 23, 32, 41, 50

6, 15, 24, 33, 42, 51

8, 17, 26, 35, 44, 53

Your destiny years

Your most important years are 5, 14, 23, 32, 41, 50, 68, 77 and 86.

GEMINI

Star Sign Compatibility

Before I met my husband, I'd never fallen in love. I'd stepped in it a few times.

—Rita Rudner

How compatible are you with your current partner, lover or friend? Did you know that astrology can reveal a whole new level of understanding between people simply by looking at their star sign and that of their partner? In this chapter I'd like to share some special insights that will help you better appreciate your strengths and challenges using Sun sign compatibility.

The Sun reflects your drive, willpower and personality. The essential qualities of two star signs blend like two pure colours, producing an entirely new colour. Relationships, similarly, produce their own emotional colours when two people interact. The following is a general guide to your romantic prospects with others and how, by knowing the astrological 'colour' of each other, the art of love can help you create a masterpiece.

When reading the following I ask you to remember that no two star signs are ever *totally* incompatible. With effort and compromise, even the most 'difficult' astrological matches can work. Don't close your mind to the full range of life's possibilities! Learning about each other and ourselves is the most important facet of astrology.

Each star sign combination is followed by the elements of those star signs and the results of their combining. For instance, Aries is a fire sign

27

and Aquarius is an air sign, and this combination produces a lot of 'hot air'. Air feeds fire and fire warms air. In fact, fire requires air. However, not all air and fire combinations work. I have included information about the different birth periods within each star sign and this will throw even more light on your prospects for a fulfilling love life with any star sign you choose.

Good luck in your search for love, and may the stars shine upon you in 2011!

Compatibility quick-reference guide

Each of the twelve star signs has a greater or lesser affinity with one another. The quick-reference guide will show you who's hot and who's not so hot as far as your relationships are concerned.

GEMINI + ARIES

Air + Fire = Hot Air

Why wouldn't the sparks fly when Gemini and Aries choose to have a relationship together? After all, you are fire and air, elementally speaking, in the astrological scheme of things. This immediately indicates a warm if not exciting relationship that will attract you to each other.

One of the key characteristics of Gemini is their incredible intellectual curiosity and ability. They love sharing ideas and this will stimulate Aries in so many ways. But this relationship is not limited entirely to intellect and will extend to your physical

Quick-reference guide: Horoscope compatibility between signs (percentage)

	Aries	Taurus	Gemini	Cancer	Leo	Virgo	Libra	Scorpio	Sagittarius	Capricorn	Aquarius	Pisces
Pisces	65	85	50	90	75	70	50	95	75	85	55	80
Aquarius	55	80	90	70	70	50	95	60	60	70	80	55
Capricorn	50	95	50	45	45	95	85	65	55	85	70	85
Sagittarius	90	50	75	55	95	70	80	80	85	55	60	75
Scorpio	80	85	60	95	75	85	85	90	85	65	60	95
Libra	70	75	90	60	65	80	80	85	80	85	95	50
Virgo	45	90	75	75	75	70	80	85	70	95	50	70
Leo	90	70	80	70	85	75	65	75	45	70	70	75
Cancer	65	80	60	75	70	75	60	95	55	45	70	90
Gemini	65	70	75	60	80	75	90	60	75	50	90	50
Taurus	65	70	70	80	70	90	75	85	50	95	80	85
Aries	60	60	70	65	90	45	70	80	90	50	55	65

and daily life as well. Overall the two of you will get on very well together.

Because Geminis sometimes tend to blow hot and cold, Aries can be useful in helping to lift you up out of the doldrums when you do feel cool. On the other hand, when you blow hot, the two of you could end up having confrontations, with you trying to outdo Aries or vice versa. This can be exciting for a while but can become problematic in a long-term relationship.

You like to think things through rationally, whereas Aries is much more impulsive. You can give them direction but their egos do tend to get a little out of hand. You'll need every ounce of cleverness to handle this part of Aries.

As a couple, your nerves could become frayed. You are not quite as physically energetic as Aries and they may like to test your stamina. At times you'll feel you've reached your breaking point with them. Your sexual relationship together could be quite playful due to the fact that you have a lot of youthful and inventive energy and you'll probably never really tire of each other.

You must remember that Aries is predominantly physical and because of your strong communicative and intellectual leanings, sometimes you may feel as if you're not quite on the same wavelength. But as I said, there's enough here in this combination to keep you sufficiently interested. Due to the fact that both of you are rather original and creative in your approaches to life, your emotional and sexual experiences together will keep your passion alive.

With Aries born between the 21st and 30th of March, a great friendship is likely to arise. Don't be surprised if this partnership becomes a red-hot love affair.

Your relationship with an Aries born between the 31st of March and the 10th of April is also an excellent one in which you both share a great mutual understanding. Furthermore, your financial and commercial relationship together means this is a good business arrangement. An understanding of each other's practical needs seems to be the cornerstone of this relationship.

By far your best choice among the Aries group is with those born between the 11th and 20th of April. Having their co-ruler Jupiter as part of their birthday mix means that they have a good chance of being highly attracted to you before becoming deeply emotional and even maritally inclined towards you. This is a great long-term combination and your romance together will be fulfilling.

GEMINI + TAURUS

Air + Earth = Dust

You are constantly racing against the clock, filling your agenda with 101 things to do. You love being busy rather than bored.

This prelude is meant to acclimatise you gently to what life with your Taurean partner may be like. Your hectic lifestyle will frustrate Taurus, and their hesitating, plodding nature will likewise challenge you by causing you to either slow down or look to greener pastures for love.

You are fast, scattered and impulsive, and this you already know by studying your Gemini characteristics. Taurus on the other hand is an earthy, practical and not so idealistic star sign. You'll need to find a balance between their fear of change and your desire to rush headlong into life and all its experiences. If the two of you can find a balance between these extremes, your ruling planets of Mercury and Venus respectively will provide for you a positive future together.

Due to these two planets being friendly in the zodiac you have a natural attraction towards each other and love spending time together. Humour, socialising and sharing your relationship with close friends brings you both tremendous joy. There is also the probability of good artistic and cultural interests that the two of you find in common.

Remember yet again that on an intimate level your fast pace may become your undoing with a Taurus partner. If you're patient enough, they will reveal their passionate, loving and loyal side to you. But particularly in the realm of romance and love, Taurus may be far happier waiting to test the water to see just what sort of partner you'll make for them, so let's not rush this one, Gemini.

In the bedroom Taurus will tantalise you if you are prepared to 'bed down' (excuse the pun) and exercise some patience until they are ready to respond to you in their naturally sensual manner, which is tactile and very erotic at times. Don't expect any quick fixes in the bedroom with your Taurus lover.

If your Taurus partner was born between the 21st and the 30th of April, expect a pretty good combination, especially where communication is concerned. But you mustn't bombard them with too many intellectual ideas. They need a few moments here and there to savour your intellectual brilliance.

A superior combination can be expected with any Taurean born between the 1st and the 10th of May. Mercury has a very powerful impact on their birthdates, which is also your ruling planet. The two of you will share many of each other's personal qualities and this experience will augment your relationship.

With those born between the 11th and the 21st of May, a steadier lifestyle can be expected. You might feel a little smothered by this possessive Taurean, but you will always know they love you.

GEMINI + GEMINI
Air + Air = Wind

Romance with the same star signs are usually fraught with a little danger. In the case of two Geminis, it's more than likely this will be a hit or miss affair.

You are both extremely nimble, active and possibly quite scattered. Therefore, bringing the two of you together requires an immense amount of discipline to make 'heads or tails' of the relationship.

Although communication is a strong point for the two of you—and this will most likely be the main source of your attraction to each other—there's every likelihood that an excess of such airy stimulation will cause this relationship to blow about aimlessly. One of you needs to step up to the plate and be the hero to give the relationship a meaningful direction.

Let's not forget that the sign of Gemini is the twin. In other words, when there are two sets of twins, the result is that there are probably four people in your relationship. Many intricate factors already have to be dealt with in a straightforward relationship, but where do we start in this case? Because Geminis are such complex personalities, teaming up with another equally complex character means there are greater challenges ahead for you.

Part of the trouble is that Gemini can be duplicitous. There is a hidden side to your nature and the two of you need to lay all your cards on the table at the outset. In other words, honesty is the best policy for you both.

You love sharing stories and coming up with new and original ideas together. These ideas might not always be practical enough to 'get legs', but you'll have a lot of fun reaching into each other's minds and seeing just how similar you are.

Humour will be the one saving grace in this relationship, particularly when things get a little out of hand. All relationships go through their ups and downs, but at least the two of you are able to laugh off some of the less-serious difficulties or differences.

Sexually you have an excellent rapport and will be very playful in each other's company. Because you know quite well what your needs are, it stands to reason that you'll instinctively understand your Gemini partner's needs as well. This can only make for a mutually satisfying sexual component to this partnership.

Your relationship with another Gemini born between the 22nd of May and the 1st of June indicates a great partnership. Your interests, both mentally and socially, are extraordinarily similar, but your opinions on things will differ considerably and therefore this forecasts a battle of egos in the future.

Your compatibility with Geminis born between the 2nd and the 12th of June is very sensual and loving by nature. You understand each other's physical needs and so your sexual expression seems to be spotlighted by this combination.

Geminis born between the 13th and the 21st of June will have some sort of karmic connection with you. Your spiritual relationship together will bring out life's deeper issues and therefore it will be a catalyst for each other's personal and spiritual growth.

GEMINI + CANCER
Air + Water = Rain

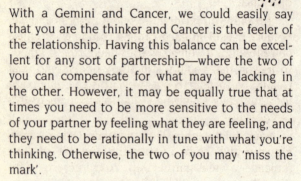

With a Gemini and Cancer, we could easily say that you are the thinker and Cancer is the feeler of the relationship. Having this balance can be excellent for any sort of partnership—where the two of you can compensate for what may be lacking in the other. However, it may be equally true that at times you need to be more sensitive to the needs of your partner by feeling what they are feeling, and they need to be rationally in tune with what you're thinking. Otherwise, the two of you may 'miss the mark'.

You must understand that Cancer is one of the most sensitive signs of the zodiac. There will be days where you will just not be able to figure out Cancer's emotional swings and why and how they react the way they do. Unfortunately, as long as you try to deal with them using your mind, you are never going to get to the bottom of what's going on.

What you need with your Cancerian partner is to develop your psychic intuition. It is worthwhile feeling—not just with your heart, but with your soul—what they need and what they are trying to say to you. The moment you enter into this path with your Cancerian friend, I can safely say you are on the road to creating a beautiful relationship with them.

You are the sort of person who prides yourself on adaptability and change, on your excitement for and experiences of life. Cancer, too, is an adaptable character but perhaps not as flighty or prone to experimentation as you are. You must always run your ideas past Cancer in a way that doesn't upset their desire for security and the comforts of home, because these things are paramount to their sense of wellbeing and inner peace.

Cancer has a wonderful ability to make you feel loved and nurtured. Being ruled by the Moon, which is the maternal archetype, you definitely feel as if you've found a soft place to land in life by engaging yourself in a Cancerian relationship. By expressing your feelings to Cancer, the intensity of your romance will blossom.

If you happen to be in a relationship or considering one with a Cancer born between the 22nd of June and the 3rd of July, there are some powerful financial considerations that are at work in the friendship. You might not be all that stimulated emotionally, but working and sharing your business ideas should be seen as stepping stones to bigger and better things on an emotional platform.

With Cancerians born between the 4th and the 13th of July, expect an intense relationship. You may need to change your outlook on life and this will come with some sort of sacrifice and certainly some challenges from your Cancerian partner.

Cancerians born between the 14th and the 23rd of July are a little less difficult to deal with and your relationship with them should be quite fulfilling. These Cancerians are also more open to your psychological and mental influence and will want to learn quite a bit from you.

GEMINI + LEO
Air + Fire = Hot Air

Here again we find the air and fire combination, which is usually a good match, astrologically. Your versatility and mental plane is attractive to Leo, who is also intelligent, social and dramatic by nature. You find them fascinating, to say the least.

The two of you will have to admit that there is a certain amount of pride involved in your choice of romantic partners. While you may have some fairly high expectations of the lover you want to be seen with, and spend your life with, it is equally if not more important for your Leo partner, one of the proudest signs of the zodiac. Having said this, you'll need to be on your best behaviour and look your finest to walk arm in arm at any social engagement with them.

If your emotional and communication compatibility is to reach a high level, you'll need to bridge the gap between Leo's huge ego and need for approval by others, and your desire to prove just how intelligent and correct you are on many issues. The two of you will be constantly trying to outdo each other. Don't take things too seriously and you should never ever react in a way which could demean or hurt or wound the pride of Leo, especially in the company of others. Remember that.

Leo is extremely loyal once they commit themselves to someone. You'll see this very quickly in their warmth, generosity and ability to amuse and attract many friends and admirers. You, with your powers of persuasion and excellent communication skills, also entice many people into your orb. Together you are a formidable couple and should be successful in many different spheres of life.

Gemini and Leo are astrologically compatible. Great friendship is the foundation of your connection, but financial and material success is also likely when you team up together. Business should prosper and your emotional relationship should be fulfilling as well.

A great deal of excitement is found between Gemini and Leo. Air is the fuel for fire and therefore you'll soon discover you naturally and instinctively trigger the passionate side of your Leo partner.

Leos born between the 24th of July and the 3rd of August are only moderately compatible with you. Things may take a while to warm up with them and you need to make an extra effort to listen to what they are saying because you may miss some of the significant hints they offer you.

A good match is likely with Leos born between the 4th and 13th of August. You'll satisfy each other's needs quite nicely. These people are very outgoing and fun to be with.

You are not likely to get on too well with Leos born between the 14th and 23rd of August. Both of you are opinionated and will try to shove your ideas down each other's throats. You may not share an entirely friendly competitiveness, either, which could result in you draining each other mentally and emotionally.

GEMINI + VIRGO
Air + Earth = Dust

Because the two of you just happen to be ruled by the same planet, Mercury, you might at first think: 'Hey, we're perfectly compatible.' However, having the same ruling planet doesn't necessarily guarantee that your compatibility rating is going to be perfect, even though it does give you some similar traits.

You need to understand that your ruling planet operates through your and Virgo's sign very differently. Firstly, with Gemini being an air sign, Mercury predominantly influences you through the realms of ideas and concepts. Virgo on the other hand is an earth sign, so Mercury conducts itself in a more pragmatic, stable and security conscious fashion.

Your and Virgo's ideas may be similar, your opinions may overlap, but at the end of the day how you execute your ideas may be very different. In particular, Virgo has an exceedingly high standard to which everyone (including themselves) must adhere. You, being a free thinker, will find that rather odd and can't handle the idea of having someone lead you around on a leash, or so it may appear to you.

Virgo is precise and may continually correct you on any number of things. This will be irritating to you and can throw you into a tailspin if you overreact to each and every comment they make. Virgo is methodical and, to your way of thinking, pretty uptight about many things, while you have a great sense of humour and are able to laugh at yourself.

Virgo has an incredible ability to serve you in a way that requires you to drop the superficiality of your mind, look deeper within and ask yourself the hard questions about life. If you are unbiased and able to see through to the motivation for their comments, your Gemini–Virgo relationship will act as an evolutionary catalyst to make you become a much greater person. Virgo is after all primarily concerned with service and support.

In the bedroom, your sexual and intimate interests will be best served by utilising your mercurial humour. Believe it or not, Virgo will identify with what you are saying and where you are coming from.

You won't always be able to compromise to reach a satisfactory conclusion with Virgos born between the 24th of August and the 2nd of September, but you'll be able to maintain a reasonably good relationship, which is the cornerstone of any good union.

In Virgos born between the 13th and 23rd of September, the influence of Venus brings to them grace, charm and a strong streak of sensuality. With them you'll feel comfortable and, furthermore, their practicality is a bonus for your material welfare. The two of you can make money together.

If you team up with a Virgo born between the 3rd and the 12th of September, you have to understand that your spiritual connection will probably supersede any other need or desire the two of you feel for each other. This is not to say you can't enjoy your mental and physical relationship together, but the spiritual component of your friendship will dominate you both.

GEMINI + LIBRA
Air + Air = Wind

You are fascinated and easily attracted to the other air sign of the zodiac, Libra. With both of you coming under the dominance of the element of air, your personalities will naturally mingle, appreciate and love each other. You are stimulated socially, intellectually and creatively by your close friendship. Therefore, this is an excellent start to something special.

Being with friends comes naturally to both of you. Air signs have the forte of communicating with people. You appreciate this in each other because you are just so good at it.

Imagination and communication will be employed in all of your dealings with each other. Neither of you is content to deal with the superficial, day-to-day humdrum of life. This is because in the middle of any activity you'll be constantly reaching for something bigger and brighter, and inspiring the other to do the same. You'll take great pleasure in seeing each other grow, and growing together.

The air signs are culturally curious, if not artistically gifted. You both seek interests that engage the more refined aspects of humanity such as philosophy, art, music and even humanitarian work, which will give you a feeling of connectedness to your fellow beings. Doing this together will also give you a sense of harmony in the relationship.

There are times when your relationship with Libra may not be so calm and peaceful. This might be when Libra is trying to find balance but may not be able to. And you, you have to admit, have moments when you are not exactly in a state of equilibrium, either. Sometimes the two of you could find it difficult to create a stable and secure day-to-day routine. You need to work on this together.

Sexually you stimulate each other tremendously. Elementally you are graded quite well astrologically and can look forward to being satisfied by your imaginative and sexually creative Libran partner. The two of you are mutually affectionate and mean it when you say you love each other.

A very lovely relationship is possible with Librans born between the 23rd of September and the 3rd of October due to the fact that Venus, the natural planet of affection, love and marriage, has a strong sway over them. These individuals are graceful, artistic and talented in many ways and also appreciate the talents that you possess.

Librans born between the 4th and 13th of October have a very zestful nature and love change and excitement. You'll feel electrified in their company due to Uranus and Aquarius, the eccentric planet and sign ruling them, along with Venus. You'll have an unsettled but exciting and spontaneous time with them.

A relationship with Librans born between the 14th and the 23rd of October is quite a good combination, astrologically. You will feel an immediate attraction to them, but please take your time to understand them deeply. You need someone who is a stabilising influence in your life and these Librans are quite the opposite.

GEMINI + SCORPIO
Air + Water = Rain

Generally people are correct when they assume Scorpios are strong, silent types. Yes, for the most part, Scorpios are secretive and uncommunicative, unless they find good reason to reveal the darker, hidden parts of their personality. And here is that exception, which is with Gemini.

Why would this be, you ask? Well, Gemini, you do have the uncanny ability of being able to somehow sow the seeds of trust with Scorpio and they in some way open up and communicate to you. And when they do, you'll be overwhelmed by the depth and breadth of their feelings. Under their sometimes icy, cold exteriors there is a seething cauldron of passion that you want to tap into.

Scorpio is not a superficial sign and, although many accuse you of superficiality, you'll find yourself in a deeper, more thoughtful mood in the company of a Scorpio partner. They demand your full attention and won't accept any compromise in their love life. For this reason you'll need to be focused and completely committed if you are to walk along the Gemini–Scorpio relationship path.

One of the other things you'll quickly learn with Scorpio is that they are masters of manipulation and understand immediately when they are being deceived because their psychic powers are profound. Don't try to beat them, deceive them, or play mind games with them. You won't win, even if you do have a superior IQ. Scorpio doesn't need an IQ to understand anything. They can just use their finely tuned 'psychic scalpel' to open up any mind that comes before them.

Scorpio is sexual in nature and, being the eighth sign of the zodiac, dominates the sensual, sexual, hidden emotional and transformative aspects of human nature. You need to be fully prepared for an intense relationship if you make a decision to join your heart with a Scorpio's heart. But if you do, the rewards will be extraordinary.

Scorpio loves like no other and will treat you to their intense emotional, mental and sexual capacities. 'Can you deal with this?' is the only question you need to be asking yourself. Scorpio is possessive but fully supportive and loyal once they give their commitment to you.

There will be some difficulty in the relationship if you choose a Scorpio born between the 24th of October and the 2nd of November. Your minds don't seem to be compatible and, although you'd like a lighter, more casual approach to life, these Scorpios are quite heavy and philosophical in nature.

Scorpios born between the 13th and the 22nd of November are also intense emotionally. You'd prefer something less deep and demanding, and therefore your whole personality may need to undergo a radical transformation to remain in a relationship with these individuals.

With Scorpios born between the 3rd and 12th of November, a lasting relationship can indeed be anticipated. These are probably the best suited to Gemini out of all the Scorpios, due to the fact that Jupiter is one of their ruling planets and strongly influences the likelihood of marriage and a prospective soulmate.

GEMINI + SAGITTARIUS
Air + Fire = Hot Air

These two signs are astrological opposites in the zodiac and will therefore attract each other quite easily. Yet again the fire of Sagittarius works well with the air of Gemini. The two of you will find much in common in your union.

Sagittarius is easygoing, fun and generous, and this appeals to your fast and curious mind. The two of you are flexible, changeable and most certainly in need of variety to keep you both personally interested in a connection with someone else.

You appreciate the fact that the Sagittarian archer is always aiming towards higher and brighter things, exploring life and keenly interested in what the world has to offer. You find it rather appealing that you could somehow be part of that journey and share your experiences with them as well.

Sagittarians are well-known travellers who have a wealth of experience with different parts of the world and other cultures. Because of your mental curiosity, this too is very appealing to you.

Sexually you are quite compatible and the elements that rule you in the zodiac stimulate one another very nicely. You feel enlightened and uplifted by the communication you share and this will extend to your physical and sexual compatibility as well.

One of the best matches can be expected with Sagittarians born between the 23rd of November and the 1st of December. Jupiter co-rules your area of relationships and love and therefore there is a natural affinity with these individuals, who are also double Sagittarians. There are moments where you marvel at their generosity and possibly even question their motives for being as open-handed as they are.

There is something frustrating about a relationship between a Gemini and Sagittarius who was born between the 2nd and the 11th of December, and the reason for this is the Mars–Aries influence on them. This makes them larger-than-life characters who tend to be wilful in their approach to life. They have an excellent way of communicating, can be very persuasive, but also sometimes self-opinionated and not at all amenable to changing their minds if you have a better way forward for them. There may be a few arguments in store for you with Sagittarians born between these dates.

Sagittarians born between the 12th and 22nd of December offer you great friendship and considerable mental stimulation. You'll feel supported by them in anything you wish to do. And this will be genuine. The strength of this relationship is in your completely open communication with each other.

GEMINI + CAPRICORN
Air + Earth = Dust

Your Gemini–Capricorn astrological match is not exactly high up on the list of best matches in the zodiac. But there is always a positive in any combination, so we don't have to throw out the baby with the bathwater too quickly.

There is a difference in both quantity and quality between Gemini and Capricorn. Gemini is fast, versatile and adaptable to modern ways of doing things. On the other hand, Capricorn is measured, slower and less wilful in their approach. To Capricorn, 'less' is sometimes 'more'.

Your Capricorn partner is particularly conventional in many areas and this can make you feel stifled, even smothered. You'd like to think that your up beat, childlike attitude would win their hearts and help propel them into a more carefree attitude and lifestyle. Well, Gemini, part of this is true and you will win them with your childlike innocence. But as for converting them into some sort of progressive modern-day 'speculators in love', that may not happen easily.

I am not saying that Capricorn can't be up to date in the way they live their lives. What I am saying, however, is that issues of security are most important to Capricorn-born individuals. Before they can let go, have fun and move with the times, they need to sew up issues of steadiness, perseverance and financial security for themselves. They'll never be comfortable letting these things slide.

If you're able to elicit trust on their part by supporting them in their ventures, you'll be totally surprised at how willing they are to meet you halfway once these needs have been met. You can satisfy their desire for security by slowing your pace a little to give them a sense that you are adaptable enough to consider their needs.

This is real love and, of course, when the gloss of passion wears off after some time, as it does with most relationships, you'll feel blessed that you have a relationship with someone who is operating from within their real self.

Capricorn is stimulated by you sexually and does feel entertained by your very playful and humorous attitude. You'll need to give them time to warm to you and express a deeper, passionate element of their nature, which is there but not always evident on first meeting.

Capricorns born between the 23rd of December and the 1st of January are not that easy for you to get on with. They have a strong Saturn influence that makes them come across as ruthless and uncaring. As far as money is concerned, you could consider them a little tight fisted. To them you may appear too easygoing and wasteful with your money. This is not a particularly good astrological match.

A relationship with a Capricorn born between the 2nd and 10th of January could work. These individuals are much more sensitive than the typical Capricorns we've been talking about and they are more creative and cultured by nature. You can find mutual interests and this will help your relationship no end. They also work reasonably well with you.

Capricorns born between the 11th and 20th of January are serious individuals and you find it hard to loosen up and be carefree with them. Why do you still feel attracted to them? At times it is difficult to explain the strange ways of love.

GEMINI + AQUARIUS
Air + Air = Wind

The Gemini–Aquarius combination is one of the most compatible in the zodiac, but also one that can be extremely challenging, too. The two of your generate high levels of energy, have ideas and desires that need to be fulfilled, and will place excessive demands on each other.

But this progressive Aquarian individual can push you in such a way that brings out your best flavours, Gemini. Once you start to see your radical transformation taking place in the company of an Aquarian, are you going to complain about it? Vice versa, your wonderful intellectual rapport and communication skills are greatly appreciated by Aquarius and they also feel that your company is good for them. The two of you do tend to bring out each other's highlights.

Aquarians are stubborn due to the fixity of their star sign, rebelling against anything that doesn't suit their way of thinking. You are a little more adaptable and could be frustrated when you give them good reasons for adjusting their opinions. They probably won't, which can make you feel as if you aren't respected for what you have to say.

You have a great interest in anything intellectual—reading, cinema, acting and other cultural pursuits—and Aquarius also is freethinking enough to enjoy the same sorts of things. There is also the added benefit of the fact that Aquarius is the sign of man, the humanitarian zodiac sign, relating to social, political and global progress. The improvement and involvement of yourselves in these processes will be a fascinating topic for Aquarians and one that will stimulate you to action, too.

Aquarians are innovators, people who make things happen. However, being ruled by the planet Uranus makes them somewhat abrupt and unpredictable. This will be unsettling to you because, even though you enjoy variety in your life, the sudden nature of the changes that often seem to visit your Aquarian friend can be a little overwhelming for your nervous system. You need to brace yourself from time to time in this relationship.

You are sexually attracted to each other and both love to flirt. Aquarians have an avant-garde, if not unconventional, manner of approaching relationships. As long as you talk about your romantic philosophies, and agree, then the relationship should fare quite well. Your sexual time together can be fulfilling.

A relationship with Aquarians born between the 21st and 30th of January has a chance of going the distance. One thing, however. They may be incorrigible flirts, which could cause you to feel jealous and insecure. This particular aspect of their personality may not sit well with you.

A special soul connection is likely with Aquarians born between the 31st of January and the 8th of February. Their sense of humour and easygoing attitude is not typical of Aquarius and is something that also attracts you.

You want to be in the company of Aquarians born between the 9th and 19th of February because Venus has a considerable say in their lives. They are sensitive, imaginative and also possess creative flair along with a strong sex appeal. This is a relationship that could offer both of you a great deal of romance.

GEMINI + PISCES
Air + Water = Rain

If you don't mind unpredictability in your relationships, then the moody, sensitive energy of Pisces won't bother you. Pisces is a water sign with connections to Neptune and to some extent the Moon. For the most part, your Piscean partner lives in a world that is completely out of view of most of us, and therefore this makes it hard for us to understand where they are coming from a lot of the time.

A Pisces is intuitive, instinctive and spontaneous. You like to think things through with your mind and, although you can be creatively spontaneous in the moment as well, the 'otherworldliness' of Pisces is hard to define. Nevertheless, there is in you a magical attraction to this mystic of the zodiac. You can indeed fall in love with Pisces.

The two of you are what are known as mutable or adaptable signs. This is good to some extent; however, too much adaptability doesn't allow for very much in the way of grounding. You need to anchor this relationship and agree to move in one direction together, if you are serious.

Your Piscean partner gives all in love. If there is any difficulty in this relationship, it is that you could find yourself playing second fiddle to their profound ability to extend love. But you mustn't let this deter you. Far from running away with your tail between your legs, why not let Pisces show you what it really means to love wholeheartedly?

From this truly spiritual connection with Pisces flows many other gifts of love and romance. Their soft, tactile and genuinely compassionate understanding will help you open your heart and share the physical side of your relationship with them. It will be easy to feel sexually satisfied knowing that your other needs are naturally being cared for and fulfilled by them.

Although your ruling planet Mercury is debilitated in the sign of Pisces, not functioning quite as well as it does in some of the other signs, there is something to be said for letting go of your rational approach to love and life and working more from the spiritual ideal. This will indeed work positively for you.

The most promising combination in a relationship with Pisces is with those born between the 20th and 28th or 29th of February. You'll be emotionally and sexually fulfilled with them if you are able to trust them. Their psychic gifts will also reveal things to you that you thought were not possible.

Pisces born between the 1st and the 10th of March are some of the most emotional in the zodiac. They can overreact to trifling matters and this in turn could make you feel distressed. Yours will not be an easy relationship.

The passionate side of Pisces is brought out in those born between the 11th and the 20th of March. Lovemaking will be the cornerstone of your relationship but you have to understand that they are also very demanding and possessive. Well, you can't have your cake and eat it, too, can you Gemini?

2011:
The Year Ahead

A man who views the world the same at 50 as he did at
20 has wasted 30 years of his life.

—Muhammad Ali

Romance and friendship

Making your dreams a reality is not always easy, even if you clearly visualise what it is you wish for in your life. At times you can clearly see the type of partner, relationship and destiny you'd hope for, but how do you make that a reality?

In 2011 Neptune, the planet of ideals and spiritual fulfilment, is at the zenith of your horoscope and as the year commences the added romantic vibrations of Venus means you can easily manifest your visualisations to make your romantic ideals come true.

You will see yourself in a new light this year. You can feel changes are imminent and actually you mustn't force destiny's hand but continue to trust the process of your life. Love is sure to find you throughout the coming twelve months, and this is particularly true for those of you who are yet to find your soulmate.

You have excellent communication skills this year (not that a Gemini is ever at a loss for words), and you are able to make a greater impact on others through the beneficial position of Mercury and the Moon. After the first week of January, Venus enters your most important romance zone, which highlights your need to find fulfilment in your relationships.

In February, the continuing influence of Venus and Neptune is a godsend. Your sexual and deeper emotional issues will be spotlighted and you will want to find out the causes of those things that so far have inhibited you in your love life.

You have a constructive approach to your relationships this month, which is due in part to the excellent relationship between Mars and Saturn. Venus also makes a formidable connection with transformative Pluto after the 10th, and this can bring you a greater awareness of not only your own concerns but those of others. Sweeten your words and you will receive an excellent response.

March is an exciting time, when Venus enters into a favourable aspect to the progressive and unpredictable Uranus, giving you plenty of social opportunities. The tried and tested won't be of interest to you as you move to take on board the philosophies and opinions of others. Try to balance the old with the new as you attempt a renovation of your life throughout this month.

You are driven by friendships in April and, when Mars enters your zone of social activities, you'll find yourself surrounded by friends, absorbed in different outings and meetings with many of them. Perhaps because Venus causes you to doubt yourself this month, you'll want some encouragement and acknowledgement from those you respect—and you'll get it. If you need to share what's going on in your mind with someone, do it only with a person whom you trust implicitly and know will not hold anything against you when you open your heart to them.

Several planets challenge Saturn's connection to your zone of love affairs in May. This particular zone of your horoscope also has a marked influence on your creative abilities. Think about this and don't be afraid to step outside your normal routine to explore avenues that will give you this sort of stimulus.

The planets will express themselves at this time through some sort of aloofness or a cooling off of your romantic feelings. Don't overplay this, however, because it's natural for all relationships to go through their peaks and troughs. The year 2011 may be one such period when, due to the opposing influences of Venus and Saturn, you may feel a little lost for a while as far as your relationships are concerned.

Jupiter, the greater benefactor of the zodiac, enters your zone of compassion, spirituality and also expenses after the 5th of June. This is a warning for you to be careful about how you approach your love life and others who mean something to you. Any sort of excessive display of generosity might backfire. Try to be yourself at this time; engage yourself in activities that give you greater insight into yourself so that you will attract only those who genuinely love you for who you are.

After the 10th of June, Venus will enter your Sun sign and this should start a new cycle for you that will restore your confidence and give you greater happiness. Along with this, a positive influence between Venus and Saturn commences, which stabilises your relationship. This will be greatly welcomed by you and your partner.

Wonderful news can be expected for many born under Gemini throughout July. It's not a well-known fact but the second zone of the horoscope along with the fourth zone has considerable influence on the family. This has more to do with acquisition and, for some of you, new additions to the family can be expected. At the very least, friends may invite you to engagements, weddings and other celebratory functions, which all add an extra dose of joy to your life during this period.

Travel is on the cards at the end of July and throughout August. These are not travels you would ordinarily have to do regarding business or other tedious issues, but more for the sheer pleasure and cultural pursuits that are often associated with social engagements.

Online romances can take place through website dating and other more modern forms of connecting with friends and lovers. Because Gemini is an intellectual and progressive sign, most of you shouldn't have too much difficulty in approaching these new methods of dating with an open mind. For those of you who are a little older, you may feel trepidation in putting your name up on what may seem to be an endless, impersonal cyberspace.

Towards the end of September you may feel a slight return of the 'love blues', which was evident earlier due to the difficult aspect between Venus and Saturn. This shouldn't last too long and, throughout October, Mars and Jupiter bring back not only your self-confidence but a big picture attitude that makes you larger than life and demanding of what you want. Your ideals can finally take shape during this cycle. Venus, Mars and Jupiter are all poised to bring you social and romantic opportunities in many different areas of your life. You need to remain open and not limit yourself to the same old routine or habits that you've utilised in the past.

You also need to avoid entangling yourself in mind games this month. You'll be concerned that your partner or someone you wish to be closer to is not as easily available as you'd like them to be. By entering into psychological games of cat and mouse, you'll only scare the person away and diminish your chances of strengthening your ties with them. Honesty and integrity are the best ways to deal with any situation that might be leaving you hanging in limbo.

During October, Venus once again makes contact with your seventh zone of marriage, love and public relations. At this time it will make an important connection with the karmic planets, indicating either a return of someone you knew in the past or a meeting with a person who seems just so familiar to you. Even if this is a perfect stranger, you'll be surprised at the deep, soulful connection you feel with each other.

Dealing with family issues may be significantly time consuming throughout November because of Mars's influence on your zone of domestic affairs. You need to make sure your diary has adequate room for those in your family whom you may have been avoiding lately or simply too busy to give enough of your attention. Deep down within yourself you'll probably be feeling a little uncomfortable. Why not kill two birds with one stone and create a situation in which friends and family can interact together? This will give you the chance to bridge the gap between your sometimes less-than-upfront social life and your more personal family situation. This event could work for all concerned and may save you a bit of time, too, because you can amalgamate these two areas of your life.

Speaking of your home life, this may also be a period when you choose to make an independent break, change your locality, or even leave a long-term domestic situation for greener pastures.

The final month of 2011 continues to be active but also a little troubling due to the intense foreground aspects of Mars, the Sun, Mercury and Neptune. Balancing your emotional ideals with the reality of your situation will take some creative intelligence on your part. The most important thing in December, however, is not to tackle your emotional life from a purely intellectual vantage point. Show the people you love that you are capable of understanding their predicament sensitively. Put yourself in the other person's shoes. By compassionately feeling what they are feeling, you give yourself the best chance of drawing your loved ones closer, as well as radically altering your perception of things in a positive way that can help you grow and bring you even greater romantic satisfaction.

Work and money

Your professional energies are at a peak as the year commences, when Venus, Mars and Jupiter all provide you sufficient momentum to achieve great things. However, it is actually in February, when Mars comes to your tenth zone of professional ambitions, that we really start to see your incredible Gemini power come into its own.

It's at this time that you are able to achieve a new position, increased status, respect and possibly even demand your 'just desserts' for previous hard work. You know you've earned some sort of recognition for what you've strived for over the past few months, and this is a time when others, including your superiors, will be more than happy to listen to what you have to say and accept your proposal. Don't shy away because this can be an extraordinarily successful turning point for you.

There are excellent financial opportunities in March, during which time Venus and Jupiter enter into a lucky aspect. Increased cash and a return of money that has been loaned, supplementary sources of income and other forms of bonuses and commissions will add to your bank balance, as well as your personal happiness.

Friends are also a great source of support at this time and may help open doors for you if you are looking for new professional opportunities.

In March and April, while you may not have the same drive that was evident earlier in the year, you will still feel comfortable enough to let your past record speak for itself, ensuring a growing success for you throughout this period until the middle of 2011.

Your confidence is evident in your work and makes you popular with your clients, co-workers and other members of the public. You may, however, need to take a break after the middle of May as Venus enters the quiet zone of your horoscope. Jupiter, too, as I mentioned in your personal yearly overview, brings you into a more behind the scenes phase after the 5th of June. And you know the old saying, 'Plan your work and then work your plan'.

You will be concerned with your future security, particularly after mid June. Venus enters your zone of finance on the 4th of July and so you'll take additional time to consider not only what you are earning, but also what you are spending, and to balance the books a little more effectively.

Jupiter from its background position favourably influences Pluto, which is transiting your eighth zone of joint finances after the 8th of July. Any money that is tied up with others will be subject to review at this time. Taxes, annuities and other investments may also need to be checked. For some of you, more creative accounting is in order. If you've not been happy with the way your tax records have been kept or your investment advisers have been directing you, now is the time to jump ship to try someone else.

You need to use some creative enterprise bargaining in August, especially in the second week. Your old methods may not be working, even though they have served you well in the past. You have to keep up with the times, increase your skills and re-educate yourself. You may seriously consider taking on some new course or educational pursuit to help further your professional ambitions.

Mars, the dynamic planet of the zodiac, moves to the third zone of study, mind and travels after the 19th of September. The educational push is still evident here and may cause you to travel far and wide to seek out solutions to issues that are puzzling you just now. Mars makes favourable influences in your zone of friendships on the 23rd. Listen to the advice others give you, especially if it is of a financial or professional nature. Don't let your ego get too big to accept that someone may just know a little more about something than you.

Siblings are also shown to be a source of concern during September and October. Although your family may sometimes approach you for financial assistance, you mustn't mix business with pleasure. If you must part with money, make sure you have some level of agreement that you can refer to in the future. There's nothing worse than money getting in the way of good relationships, particularly family ones.

Be careful not to waste your money in October. The Mars–Jupiter aspect is an ominous one, indicating that you might overvalue something or possibly even lose on a gamble. Informed decisions are essential if you're not to forfeit money throughout this month. Professional advice may help you to make a judicious decision.

Throughout November the influences of the planets again seem to be hinting at family and property matters. You need to take control of these issues, whether it is by extricating yourself from meddling in family affairs or perhaps by selling property and consolidating your loans at this time.

The final month of the year has a speculative turn about it, with Venus creating excellent aspects around the 6th, 17th and the 21st. Utilise these times to make wise investments that will in the future give you an excellent return on your money.

Karma, luck and meditation

Mars enters the important karmic ninth zone of your horoscope on the 16th of January, signalling good luck through your hard work. Mars for you is a planet relating to service; your offerings to others. Therefore, believe it or not, by helping others, particularly in the first part of the year, you'll achieve some outstanding results that you wouldn't have dreamt of in the past.

Luck in your relationships is seen through the movement of Venus within the positive areas of your zodiac. In the early part of January, again after March and yet again in May, this planet influences you favourably and you can expect good fortune to shine upon you in the form of friendship, lovers and possibly even soulmates.

Your spiritual activities are highlighted with Jupiter's movement through your twelfth zone. This is an important transit and occurs once every twelve years. You may like to think that luck comes in the form of money, people or job opportunities. However, the transit of Jupiter in this position high-lights the fact that your inner life, attitudes, thinking processes and spiritual aura are the secrets to all success. By getting these parts of your being right, everything else will fall into place. Don't neglect this process, even though at first it may seem unusual to you to be indrawn, separated from others and possibly even alone for a while.

Once again Venus enters your zone of marriage after the 2nd of November. Meeting people through work, or inviting your lover or spouse to have a say in your business activities, may indeed help you achieve even greater success. If someone has some-thing to offer you by way of advice, listen carefully because this may have a radically positive influence on your activities and bring you greater life aware-ness and good fortune. Here's hoping the stars shine upon you in 2011!

GEMINI

Your Bonus 2010
Three Month
Forecast

OCTOBER 2010

Highlights of the month

You sometimes have to be cruel to be kind and in the case of older family members this will be obvious this month. Someone may not be listening to you and it may be time for you to take full control and handle the matter once and for all. This is likely between the 3rd and the 7th when the people around you are not really seeing what needs to be done. You may seem like the cruel and heartless individual in the scenario but you will eventually be thanked for taking the helm of the ship and steering it to a safe harbour.

A more entertaining and fun time can be expected from the 10th till the 15th. Plenty of entertainment is on the cards with parties and other social events cramming your diary. It's also likely you'll feel more zest and vigour for life and will find yourself in the midst of a younger group of people. There may be the possibility of meeting someone who can help further your creative interests or some work project.

After the 20th, your organisational skills and discipline will pick up and your employer may temporarily give you the opportunity to prove just how capable you are in a more senior role in your work.

You've come through some of the earlier challenges of the year and have dedicated yourself to a sustained effort that will now make life much easier for you. This is a strengthening time and one in which your confidence emerges even more strongly.

By the 26th, a discussion you have with someone may open your eyes as to the cause of some lingering health concern that you had. At first, you may not clearly relate the causes with the symptoms but deeper reflection will prove this person correct. By knowing what the issue is or, more importantly, what the causes are, you can eliminate those from your life and look forward to improved health and vitality.

Between the 27th and the 31st, you must make sure that all your communications are checked and rechecked. Spelling or grammatical errors may result in misunderstandings that can cost you financially. Double-check your meeting times or places of engagement, as sudden changes in plan may be overlooked or not conveyed to one or other parties. Keep your communication consistent and try not to let minor irritations get the better of you.

Romance and friendship

Between the 1st and the 4th, you may end up on a blind date or meeting someone who is interested in you but you may not feel quite comfortable enough to share your feelings with them. Remain calm, cool and collected in the way you express yourself. There's no need to reach the finishing line yesterday.

If you've been feeling as if you're under the thumb of someone, dominated and not quite in control of your own life, the period of the 10th till the 15th is an important cycle in which you can assert yourself again and finally break free of that person. It's time to live on your terms.

It will be time to resume a hobby that you'd put to the side a while ago, but to do so means a sacrifice in some other area of your life. Put aside your duties, share the load with some of the other family members, and dare to resume your passion and love. This can take place between the 19th and the 22nd.

If travel is something that you've also postponed, you might like to pull out those brochures and make some enquiries as to some interesting worldwide destinations. By the 25th you'll have your eye and your heart set on somewhere exotic, romantic and well within the reach of your budget.

Mars enters your zone of marriage and partnerships on the 28th, bringing with it a dose of spice, if not contention.

Smooth relations and great communications take place around the 29th till the 31st of October. You'll find yourself in the company of some beautiful people who will also make you feel equally as wonderful.

Work and money

Discussions are intense and profuse around the 3rd and the 4th. You may make a point but, particularly if you're involved in public relations or a sales-oriented business, you might actually lose the customer rather than convincing them of your viewpoint. Try to say less and you'll have a better chance of sealing up the deal.

You'll be able to curtail your expenses between the 8th and the 15th. Venus moves into retrogression so this is actually a great period to learn from your past errors and become more frugal with your finances.

Take the pressure off by enjoying yourself at work around the 19th and 20th. You can feel inspired and bring a touch of creativity, art and even music into your work place. This will soothe your frazzled nerves and make you far more productive.

New techniques and systems for improving things generally in your professional life take place between the 21st and the 24th. There may be consultants or other trainers brought in to help you learn new methodologies. Education for the purposes of improving your professional abilities and communication skills will be plentiful up till the 27th.

The comments of a work colleague or client will inspire you around the 28th. Take their advice.

Destiny dates

Positive: 8, 9, 19, 20, 21, 22, 23, 24, 25, 26
Negative: 5, 6, 7, 27
Mixed: 1, 2, 3, 4, 10, 11, 12, 13, 14, 15, 28, 29, 30, 31

Highlights of the month

No less than four planets are retrograde, meaning they're going over old ground in many areas of your life. This is necessary to make sure that the decisions you are contemplating are not based on false assumptions or faulty knowledge. In particular, Mars moving through your zone of marriage and public relations indicates that it is worth your while to double-check everything before opening your mouth. Mars is prone to misunderstandings and your relationships can take on a more competitive or aggressive edge during this phase of the year.

From the 1st till the 5th, there may be some power struggle; a desire for one of you to dominate the other in your personal life. Unless compromises are reached, this could be a difficult time that will cause your blood to boil over.

A romantic attachment is likely to arise in your workplace or with someone you least expect this month. The period of the 9th till the 15th of November is particularly highlighted for these matters. You need to be clear in your intentions and also ask the other person to state their case. Initially, this may all be guesswork and superimposing of your feelings on each other. This could make it awfully difficult to work, with your concentration levels being deluded by the distraction of loving eyes staring at you from the far corner of the office. Yes, it's best to get things straight and make sure that your romantic feelings for a co-worker don't interfere with your productivity or, worse still, your reputation.

Between the 21st and the 24th, you will react a little too hastily and thereby need to retract your statements. If you're working in the capacity of an advisor, counselling others or mediating between opposing parties, this will take on even greater significance because what you say will affect their decisions.

There are times when fashion and self-beauty can be taken to the extreme; the period of the 27th till the 30th is one such time. Some of you may have contemplated cosmetic surgery or procedures that are rather radical in the hope of making yourself look younger and more appealing. By all means do it but, in repeating the advice I've given in several predictions this year, I say please get a second opinion and additional advice before going ahead.

Romance and friendship

There's something discomforting about someone who tries too hard in love. You mustn't make too many attempts or smother your partner because desperation is the last thing a prospective lover will be attracted to between the 2nd and the 5th.

Are you still trying to keep up with friends in the lifestyle department? This may be a recurring theme this year. That's not a good idea and, in fact, it's a sure path to depression if they keep one-upping you. Between the 5th and the 10th, try to remain content within yourself and the circumstances you happen to be in your life. That's a challenge, but challenge enough. This attitude of mind will bring you more happiness than the designer label outfit your friend is wearing.

You're constructive in working through relationship issues between the 16th and the 18th. Try to be realistic about what you expect from another person and if the demands for improvement require a lot of work, why not break these down into digestible parts so that your counterpart can actually achieve what is expected of them? If you demand too much change too soon it won't happen at all.

You'll quite likely catch someone out in a white lie sometime around the 21st. Some secrets will be revealed and it may take a delicate balancing act to maintain cordial relations with them and the third parties involved. Is any of this your business, anyhow? Don't complicate the issue by sharing this information with anyone else. You could be branded a gossipmonger.

Between the 22nd and the 28th you have the floor! You can shine among your peers and make a bold statement about who you are without any ramifications whatsoever. You can exude confidence and this may have a lot to do with your choice of colours and jewellery.

Work and money

You may be performing your professional tasks excellently but could also doubt your role in the scheme of things. Between the 3rd and the 5th, you may need to re-examine your identity as a worker, as a contributor to the organisation you work for. This is all great stuff because it can help you reappraise your methods and adjust to bigger and better things.

You might be disappointed by the decision of a work colleague between the 6th and the 9th. This could be something associated with business or money and wasn't intended to hurt you in any way. You could be taking this matter far too personally. Let this slide so it doesn't interfere with what is otherwise a fairly good working relationship.

The fortunate planets, Jupiter and Venus, both go direct in their motion on the 19th, indicating a turning around for you in many areas of your life, particularly in your career and financial matters. Don't let overconfidence get the better of you.

Cut back waste on the 30th, otherwise you could get a rap on the knuckles for not being more attentive to the environmental issues at hand.

Destiny dates

Positive: 11, 12, 13, 14, 15, 16, 17, 18, 19, 25, 26
Negative: 1, 2, 21
Mixed: 3, 4, 5, 6, 7, 8, 9, 10, 22, 23, 24, 27, 28, 29, 30

DECEMBER
2010

Highlights of the month

The final month of the year promises to be both challenging and also somewhat frustrating. You may have plans and desires for your partner and yourself only to find that any suggestions you make are met with resistance, especially between the 1st and the 3rd. It's not a bad idea to communicate your intention before surprising someone. You might feel jaded buying a gift or organising an outing only to find that the response is less than lukewarm. Put the feelers out before investing emotional or financial resources so that you're not disappointed.

Your sexual energies are strong in the last month of 2010 as both Mercury and Mars trigger your carnal and lustful instincts to the max. Between the 6th and the 13th, you may find it hard reconciling these primal urges with what's been expected of you and how you've presented yourself in the past. You mustn't take yourself too seriously and try to incorporate a little bit of fun in this dramatic play of energies.

Between the 14th and the 18th, you might find the temptation to do something you wouldn't ordinarily do too hard to resist. Perhaps you'll find yourself in the company of a new group of people who are less inhibited and more prone to experimentation with new kinds of activities. It's very likely you'll want to indulge your fantasies and do something that would have shocked you years ago. But this too will be part of your learning curve and, as long as you don't let guilt get the better of you, it may be something you might be able to control.

From the 19th till the 25th, you must slow your pace because the complex aspect between Mars and the Sun makes you rash and accident-prone. There's a certain level of aggravation that may be hard for you to contain or to pinpoint. Direct action will be your favoured choice but may not yield the positive results you would hope for.

On the home front, this period requires you to be less demanding, particularly with youngsters. If you've let bad feelings build up over a period of time, this could be an explosive few days and it's not really the best time to vent your spleen with Christmas around the corner.

Making adjustments and finetuning your schedule for others for the sake of keeping the peace will be necessary between the 26th and the 31st. Eating a little humble pie will make sense to you, particularly as you'll be involved with a multitude of characters, all of whom may be too complex to balance under the circumstances.

By biting your tongue, you'll find that this will go a long way towards providing you with a peaceful conclusion to 2010.

Romance and friendship

Boring relationship? The Sun and Mars will see to it that your love life is anything *but* between the 1st and the 4th. These planets activate your level of discussion and interaction but may also rile you up. You and your partner could be at loggerheads over trifling matters on the home front. Control and moderation will be the key words.

You will require a balance between sensitivity, sentimentality and straight-up-and-down facts when you're dealing with friends on the 14th. You mustn't let your emotions get in the way of your negotiations because others will then see you as a pushover. You can continue to be direct but at the same time quietly assertive in the way you manage your friendships.

Your friends and family members want to dictate the course of events between the 18th and the 21st, but you mustn't let them do that. They could be confused and erratic in their own lives and, if you let them, this same pattern could wash over into your life. It's you who needs to run your show, on your terms, not theirs. Be strong and demand respect from everyone in the last month of the year.

With the Sun entering your zone of joint resources on the 22nd, it's quite likely that some serious discussions will take place surrounding how you are dealing with your finances. Try not to let these financial matters muddy the season's festivities. Postpone any talk of money and material differences until the new year.

Christmas will be a productive period, with Mars creating great aspects to your planets. This indicates a vibrant, up-beat and festive period for you. Take some care around the 30th when Mars and Saturn enter into a conflicting aspect, which may cause you some additional frustration, especially with youngsters.

Work and money

You'll be making an extra effort between the 1st and the 4th, given that it's the last month of the year. You could be following too many lines of thought at once for your own good, so stick to one path of action, even if others would have you believe that an alternative is better.

Have you got the right credentials to do what it is you want to do in life? You'll be thinking carefully along these lines so that you can improve your income and make the coming years more financially viable for yourself. You'll contemplate some new study course or perhaps even enrol in an educational institution between the 5th and the 8th.

Competitive energies heat up between the 16th and the 20th and you'll need to protect your turf to prove your worth. You need to channel your impulsiveness, and be patient and dedicated to the task at hand. Yet again, you'll be called upon to explain what your purpose or function in life is and, if you haven't thought about this, this last month of 2010 will bring these matters to the fore.

Pull all your financial resources together around the 22nd. Open a new bank account or transfer your savings to a higher-yielding investment.

The year 2010 finishes on a very financial note, but this should make you feel good as Jupiter continues to give you benefits on the work front for several more weeks.

Destiny dates

Positive: 1, 2, 3, 4, 5

Negative: 15, 16, 17, 18, 19, 20, 21, 23, 24, 25

Mixed: 6, 7, 8, 9, 10, 11, 12, 13, 14, 22, 26, 27, 28, 29, 30, 31

GEMINI

2011:
Month by Month
Predictions

> Do you know the difference between education and
> experience? Education is when you read the fine print;
> experience is what you get when you don't.

—Pete Seeger

Highlights of the month

This is a time of great energy and transformation
with Mars, the Sun and Pluto activating your deeper
energies. Up until the 15th you'll be re-appraising
financial transactions as well as the deeper and more
mysterious paths of life.

Try to avoid arguments with others when it
comes to your business transactions. You are
likely to be very energetic and impatient at the
same time. Don't let your desire for success blind
you to acts of human kindness.

Travel, higher education and practical spiritual
endeavours are indicated by the transit of Mars
in your ninth house after the 14th. You'll be quite
assertive and it is probably not a bad idea to take
some time out.

You'll want to exercise your constructive energies this month and therefore steady progress is likely due to the influence of Saturn. Try to remember the lessons of your past as you endeavour to deal with the emerging issues in both your work and your relationships, especially after the 24th. Venus will indeed give you plenty of charm and special ability but you also need to put your money where your mouth is and commit to a course of action.

It could be a great time to enrol in some new form of education. You're looking to make this year one in which your achievements stand out, and education could serve you well in gaining some more credentials even through some short courses.

You'll want to learn some new lessons in love this year, too, and throughout January you have ample opportunity to do so. However, you mustn't rest on your laurels in this regard, meaning you may need to include changing your personal habits, grooming and even your appearance to make things work better for you.

After the 22nd, an excellent dose of lucky Jupiter energy endows you with new opportunities to succour great friendships and also to settle old scores in a peaceful manner. This is a good time for you to set down some clear goals for your personal and social lives.

Get together with a group of friends, reassert your cultural, spiritual or even political interests and align yourself with those of similar thoughts. You may be active in spearheading some new group or movement that delves into social, cultural or humanitarian purposes. This could also be part of this whole educational thread that I see emerging for Gemini in 2011.

The latter part of January is excellent for enhancing your public image, but don't let Mars make you too aggressive in the process of doing so. Towards the 31st you may be out of step with those in your environment. Listen a little more than you speak so you can let others take the lead and thereby make a lasting impression.

Romance and friendship

Your mind is on matters of love on the 1st, and by the 3rd you can feel comfortable in discussing some minor issue with the one dearest to you. Your communication will be clear and concise and you'll receive the response that you so desire.

Between the 4th and the 6th new information comes to light and deep emotional issues are uncovered and dealt with, both within yourself and with the one you love most. For those of you who are married, this could be a breakthrough in the way you deal with each other and there is a chance to improve your relationship.

Between the 8th and the 10th, your career will interfere with your emotional or romantic involvements. Divided loyalties play havoc with your life and you need to choose one over the other.

Friendships are strong and you have the support of others between the 11th and the 13th; although around the 14th, you'll feel a little low-key and will want to spend time alone.

You're in your own element between the 15th and the 17th. Pamper yourself. Ask for what you feel you deserve and don't take no for an answer.

On the 22nd and the 23rd you'll be housebound, but this is probably just what the doctor ordered. Generously spend your time with your partner, your children and other relatives. A family reunion is likely.

Between the 24th and the 26th you'll need to sacrifice your time for those close to you. You may begrudge doing this, but something good will come out of it, so enter into your obligations with a willingness and loving sense of purpose.

Between the 28th and the 31st you may be invited to take part in a fun event. Offer your services in this arena as well, because some new opportunity or meeting may take place as a result.

Work and money

It's all about striking up a deal between the 1st and the 5th. Don't be afraid to put forward your requests, and if necessary, do so in writing. It's important to be able to verify everything that's said at this time.

Your educational pursuits between the 6th and the 11th are excellent for furthering your professional opportunities. You mustn't be stuck in the past, but continue to look upward and forward, and this may involve honing your skills and your abilities.

Between the 13th and 18th, accounting, dealing with bureaucrats and other 'number crunchers' will occupy much of your time. Be ready with the facts if you need to attend an important meeting.

You can acquire some additional cash or possibly approach your employers for increased income or bonuses between the 19th and the 23rd. Plan your approach, however, as you'll need to have justification for asking for those additional dollars.

From the 24th to the 31st, use your creative ability to push forward a project or an idea. You'll have the support of your co-workers.

Destiny dates

Positive: 1, 2, 3, 4, 5, 6, 7, 11, 12, 27, 28, 29, 30, 31
Negative: 14, 18, 19, 20, 21
Mixed: 8, 9, 10, 13, 15, 16, 17, 22, 23, 24, 25, 26

FEBRUARY 2011

Highlights of the month

It's best for you to plan carefully how you are going to spend your money this month, especially with Venus moving through your zone of shared resources. After the 4th you may overspend on something that is not at all to the liking of your partner. Do some window-shopping or online comparisons before committing yourself to any sort of big-ticket items.

Between the 10th and 13th you have an excellent opportunity for sharing your ideas and making an impact on employers and others who are capable of helping you move forward in life.

You'll have an affinity with older members of the community or family and may even be keenly interested in learning from their experiences. Taking some time out from your normal clique of friends to associate with these older individuals could benefit you immensely.

Sometime around the 19th, try to avoid head-on confrontations with others who are not at all amenable to your way of seeing and doing things. If you keep your centre of balance, are polite and listen attentively to what is said, you'll gain the respect of others and may even be able to turn things around to your advantage.

The Sun and Mercury enter your zone of career around the 20th, and this is excellent for impressing your employers, enhancing your reputation and finding renewed purpose in your work. The Sun in this position allows you to shine as a leader, albeit temporarily, by taking the helm and showing your true mettle.

You may need to deal with government, people in authority or those who may be in a position to resolve some of your personal issues associated with legal matters. After the 22nd you'll need to exercise patience to cut through a lot of the red tape, but once you've resolved some of these matters, you'll feel much better and be ready to move forward.

Making up for lost time is likely between the 23rd and 26th. Allocate some time to research your topics of interest. Don't be afraid to say no to an invitation if, instead, it means finishing a job that has been left half done. You'll be much more satisfied by disciplining yourself during this cycle. What you do and how you do it will have some significant effect on direction in the coming months. The results will speak for themselves.

Mars again in your zone of work activates the final few days of the month. Try not to oppose those who are in a position of authority. Speak your piece but let them take the lead and, where necessary, demonstrate some humility. This will keep everyone on side and is ultimately in your best interests.

Romance and friendship

You are saturated with thoughts of romance between the 1st and the 4th and you'll be wondering whether any of those paperback novels you've ever read are likely to come true in your life. Well, the answer is that it's quite likely to happen during this cycle.

Don't let your family disable you between the 7th and the 9th, however. Someone within the ranks of your domestic sphere may feel a little envious of the fact that you have created a wonderful social network and this could be causing them problems. This is a case of possessiveness on their part.

Between the 10th and the 12th, avoid fatal attractions. You may feel as if someone is perfect only to realise later that their lives are way too complicated to warrant getting involved with them. You may be being a little too subjective and not looking at the whole picture.

You'll feel flattered by an unsolicited advance around the 15th. But the question is, is this person right for you? You need to hold fast to your values and consider the repercussions of getting involved with people, especially if you know very little about them. Don't 'fall asleep at the wheel' on the journey of your life.

From the 18th till the 21st you make some worthwhile new connections. Watch your health on the 22nd, however, as you may be so overwhelmed by excitement that you forget to look after yourself. Rest a little more so that you can fully enjoy what's on offer socially.

About the 24th you'll feel really hip about how you look and you'll note that others are paying attention to you. By the 27th you'll be able to assert yourself and commence a brand new phase romantically.

Work and money

You are thinking about financial matters between the 1st and the 5th. You need to be precise in the way you tread the monetary path in the first few days of February.

You can splurge on yourself after the 8th due to the excellent aspect of Venus in your zone of shared finances. Manage your books in a way that's in keeping with this century's approaches. By all means, enjoy the way you spend, but remember you can do this wisely by claiming certain expenses and legitimate business offsets.

New opportunities open up for you between the 13th and the 20th. Carefully reassess your path and be judicious when comparing yourself with others. Jealousy is not the way to go just now. You can learn from others' standards and apply them to your own work ethic.

On the 22nd, don't be angry at the counsel you receive. It may expose some of your flaws or deficiencies. Take this as a blessing in disguise because it can only serve to make you better.

Destiny dates

Positive: 13, 14, 15, 16, 17, 18, 21, 27

Negative: Nil

Mixed: 1, 2, 3, 4, 5, 7, 8, 9, 10, 11, 12, 19, 20, 22, 23, 24, 25, 26

Highlights of the month

You are upbeat this month and people will notice it. Venus and Uranus make you electric, attractive and the centre of attention. If you are offered a date, if someone wants to introduce you to a new circle of friends, or if you have a sense that it is time to change your job, this could be the opportunity to make a significant impact on those with whom you come in contact. However, you must fight against the temptation to overdo things. These influences are strong between the 2nd and 7th.

Sometime after the 6th you'll invite the challenges that come your way and see them as a means of strengthening yourself and your resolve. Teachers, gurus and others who are in a position to help with your spirits will also be of use to you.

Some disruption to your social circle occurs after the 12th. This may not necessarily be a bad thing for you but may shed light on the circumstances surrounding one or another of your existing friends.

Your relationships are secure and stable after the 15th. Although there may be a little less excitement in your personal relationships, you'll welcome the fact that you are clear on who you are, who the other person is and what you expect from the relationship.

You are lucky after the 17th with Jupiter bringing you some unexpected good news, gifts or opportunities. Someone close to you tells you a secret that pleases you. This is not gossip but something of value; something that you can utilise as wisdom in your life.

There is also now an opportunity for you to break free of some situation that has shackled you in the past. This could also be linked to the changes in your social life, mentioned previously. Communications are excellent after the 20th and this is also a wonderful time to take a holiday, activate your physical energies by getting into some new sport or signing up to a gym.

When Venus passes through your tenth house after the 27th your reputation is again on the rise. You may make some important connections at this time and may even come under the wing of someone who has had their eye on you for a while and wishes to help you succeed. Far from being suspicious of their motives I suggest you listen carefully to what they have to say. You may be taken into a wider and more influential circle of people during this time and your sense of self-worth will definitely increase.

In the last few days of the month you must not let your pride get in the way of asking for help if your work is becoming a bit too much to handle.

Romance and friendship

Are you fully satisfied in your love life? Sometimes you need to rake up a little bit of muck. It's good for the system, Gemini! Between the 1st and the 4th you have an opportunity to lay out your cards on the table, speak your mind, and get rid of some of the excess internal baggage. You'll also be demanding that your significant other do the same.

Your identity is strong between the 5th and the 7th. You'll be breaking free of some of the limitations that you've experienced in your life and connecting with potential newcomers by browsing online or simply perusing your social life.

You'll be agreeable with others around the 11th because your manner seems pleasing and you're able to accentuate similarities rather than differences between you and them. You may have to restart some relationship after the 12th. However, the onus is on you to take the first step because pride may have stepped in the road of you getting together.

An interruption to your friendships and social activities is likely between the 16th and the 21st. You need to make sure that your arrangements are clear and concise, using open lines of communication. Not stressing the truth about how your time and effort is affected, and saying 'yes' to too many people during this stretch of time might seem delicious fun at first, but you'll soon strike problems when you realise you're short on minutes.

Someone you join up with between the 22nd and the 25th might feel as though they are entitled to be more familiar with you than they should be. You'll take this as a blatant affront and might have to say something to them. Nevertheless, you'll be surprised and possibly even secretly flattered.

Rest is mandatory on the 31st. If you have to take time out from your gruesome routine, do so. It's all about rewarding yourself, especially when you're getting ready to start a new month.

Work and money

If you're feeling imprisoned, partitioned from your friends and lovers because of work constraints between the 1st and the 10th, you need to look at the bright side and make a note of all of the positives. Being level-headed is critical at this time, so please emphasise the good, not the bad.

You'll be pleased at a disruption that occurs around the 7th. It'll give you time to breathe and collect your energies and reassert the direction in which you wish to move.

You need to remain neutral between the 9th and the 12th. Several warring factions may try to elicit your support for their cause but you'll only become corrupt and hurt by playing that game.

If you're concerned about certain boundaries in your workplace, you have a perfect opportunity to put forward your view creatively and set the record straight around the 15th. Your input will be valuable, so don't worry if you feel as if you're overstepping the bounds of your duty or responsibilities in this area. You'll win friends and respect by throwing your hat in the ring.

Finally, between the 27th and the 31st you can turn something mundane into something glorious and magical. It's all in your attitude and approach. Implement your ideas boldly at this time.

Destiny dates

Positive: 15, 22, 23, 24, 25, 27, 28, 29, 30

Negative: 8

Mixed: 1, 2, 3, 4, 5, 6, 7, 9, 10, 11, 12, 16, 17, 18, 19, 20, 21, 31

Highlights of the month

The key issue this month is working as a team member, especially from the 1st to the 5th. If you honestly appraise your choice of friends, scrutinise their behaviour and character in an unbiased fashion, you'll more than likely realise you haven't exactly made the best of choices in each and every case. You need to be careful not to tread the wrong path this month.

One of the luckiest combinations is the Jupiter–Sun relationship and, after the 13th, you'll experience the benefits of these lovely zodiacal vibrations on your life. Benefits may or may not come to you in the form of material acquisitions but could manifest as kind words or spiritual compassion from someone around you.

Generally it is believed that this combination is lucky for your financial circumstances, but it may also bring you a favourable resolution in such things as legal matters or other long and difficult monetary battles. If, for example, you've been in an unfortunate relationship that has ended in divorce or some acrimonious financial tangle, things will work out in your favour during this cycle.

This is the month to make your dreams finally come true. As Neptune slowly makes its way through your professional zone, you need to have the courage of your convictions and act upon your beliefs. You may have some sort of notion that what you wish to achieve is not doable. You need to act in confidence and believe that you can make things happen. Make these dreams a reality and don't be afraid to share the vision with others whom you know will support and assist you in bringing together all the elements to make it true.

After the 20th the Sun moves into the zone of your horoscope indicating endings. At this time you must be gracious enough to let someone or something go. It is only after creating this vacuum, a new and open space, that the universe will be able to provide you with some other exciting opportunities.

When Venus enters your eleventh house of profits on the 21st of April you will see an increase in your finances, or at least see the light at the end of the tunnel. It may not simply be because you have worked harder but possibly because you have been a little smarter in your approach and drawn the right sort of people into your orb.

Love can grow under this transit, too, and the friends you have will support you in your romantic endeavours. You need to be persistent and not fob off an invitation. Take every offer seriously, even if it doesn't work out. At this time it's a numbers game, so the more opportunities presented to you, the more you should investigate what's available to make the most of what the planets are offering you just now.

Romance and friendship

Please reassert the fact that love and friendship are sacred between the 2nd and the 4th. Discard crude, albeit novel, situations that don't add any spiritual charm to the relationships that you seek.

After the 7th you should be ready with a counter example to someone who is challenging you. You can do this in a loving and gentle manner. You realise that they need a lesson in life and you're ready to give it to them.

Where is your favourite vacation spot? Around the 12th, travel somewhere, even if it's informal and spontaneous. You need a spark in your life just now to bring you back into tender synchronisation with life's beauty.

Family matters take precedence between the 14th and the 16th. Something unexpected on the home front is fun. Share the good times with your loved ones and in particular your children. One of your kids, if you have children, could be in hot pursuit of something that's not going to serve their best interests. You need to be clever in how you point that out to them.

By the 18th there's no point becoming an injured star. Proving yourself to be invincible could end up costing you severely. Be moderate in everything you do.

Fiery communications and love blend well to give you a blast after the 22nd. You feel tension but at the same time are fully alive by these energies. You feel cheeky but your stimulation should also be measured so as not to overstep the bounds of good taste.

You receive a fair return for your emotional investment from the 27th to the 29th. Someone you love appears to be far more amorous than they usually are. Why not make hay while the sun shines.

Work and money

You could feel like a hidden passenger at your work between the 2nd and the 4th. But why not see that as a lucky break, to have a few super days without anyone bothering you? Keep to yourself and you'll get so much more done.

You have to interpret some of the clues that are being offered to you between the 5th and the 8th. Someone is looking up to you as a mentor or an implied master who maybe has some answers for them. You mustn't assume to know more than you do because this could get you in hot water.

After the 12th, someone will organise a lecture or meeting that gives you the opportunity to voice your displeasure at someone's 'dictatorship' in your workplace. Believe it or not, an insult could be advantageous in the long run and will precipitate some change.

Overspending your money is retail suicide after the 20th. Balance your incoming and outgoing cash flow so that you don't die of a heart attack when your credit card bill arrives.

Destiny dates

Positive: 6, 8, 12, 13, 14, 15, 16, 21, 22, 27, 28, 29

Negative: 18, 20

Mixed: 1, 2, 3, 4, 5, 7

MAY 2011

Highlights of the month

It's quite likely you will get a lucky financial break throughout May, but it is imperative you don't waste these valuable opportunities through excessive expenditure or overconfidence. Before you start spending, try to consolidate your position and this way you can build up a small nest egg.

Between the 1st and the 10th, those in a position of authority are receptive to your requests. Before approaching them, however, why not take a little time out to plan your approach to them carefully? Around the 11th, Mars will move to your zone of secrets. This gives you an opportunity to manoeuvre behind the scenes secretly to elicit the help you need to achieve what's on the top of your agenda.

Venus also enters this private zone on the 16th, indicating there is a lot going on beneath the surface. It's important that diplomacy takes precedence in your dealings with others. Words and actions may be misconstrued at this time.

The gossip around you is hot and tempting to take onboard, but you must resist and avoid anything that is underhanded. Use your position of trust with honour. Don't transgress against others even if initially it seems to give you the edge.

Your creative impulses become stronger and stronger between the 17th and the 22nd. Carefully blend some of your social activities with work-related matters. Don't be too serious about your success, or about yourself. Have a laugh and be prepared to laugh at yourself with others, particularly if it is all simply in good fun.

Around the 23rd, Venus and Pluto bring to the fore an aspect of your obsessive nature. You may be like a dog with a bone with a relationship. Be careful not to wear out your welcome and, if you happen to meet someone at this time, let them take the lead. Don't exhibit compulsiveness or an incessant need to be in contact with them too much. Indeed, one of the primary laws of interpersonal power is that absence makes the heart grow fonder. This scarcity principle must be utilised to maximum benefit in the area of love, and friendships as well. By stepping back, making yourself conspicuously absent from time to time, you will make others desire you more. Remember that.

Finally, in the last few days of May the conjunction of Venus and Mars brings with it intense sexual feelings and possibly impulsive actions that may be hard to overcome. Maintain a sober attitude, particularly if you are out and about, meeting new people and subject to intoxicants or other forms of pleasure. There will be a distinct tendency to overdo things, and the last thing you want is to wake up in a 'bed of regrets' the following morning.

Romance and friendship

You'll experience a comfortable period in your friendships between the 1st and the 3rd. Venus and Jupiter provide you with a sense of wellbeing and you can share this with someone close to you.

If it's that time of the year when an anniversary or special occasion arises you can take time out and enjoy the company of loved ones. Give yourself permission to get away from it all between the 4th and the 6th.

You're a little bit scattered in your communication from the 7th till the 11th. So collect your thoughts and don't try to do or say too much. The last thing you want is for people to misinterpret what your intentions are.

Feeling sentimental and safe all at the same time will be high on your list of priorities between the 12th and the 16th. You want to communicate and receive nurturing feelings during this cycle. Co-ordinate your activities with your spouse or partner and don't give them any sort of ambiguous messages. You have much more in common than you think.

From the 18th till the 21st you can further contribute to your mutual wellbeing by involving yourselves in physical activities that release stress and reset your personal perspectives in a clearer format. Making peace and moving in the same direction is important to stimulate your sense of confidence and success in your partnership.

If you're feeling lethargic in the way you approach your friendships around the 23rd, you may need a dose of caffeine to bring you back up, so to speak, to resuscitate you. You won't want to miss out on any of the social events that are presented to you leading up to the 29th.

Dealing with the misfortune of a friend on the 29th and the 31st is also spotlighted. Dedicate some time to helping them get through their difficult period.

Work and money

You are full of energy and drive after the 1st. Mars and Jupiter inject you with enthusiasm and a can-do attitude. This may be short-lived, however, as the Moon transits your quiet zone of rest on the 2nd.

Pace yourself in all matters, particularly your work. You're emotional about money between the 7th and the 11th and may need to spend more than you earn. Speculation is rife between the 14th and the 16th. Test the water first before putting all your eggs in one basket.

You are demanding of others, but respected, and can obtain a good position of authority from the 22nd till the 29th. However, give respect equally as much as you demand it. Any imbalance in this area of your life will come back to haunt you. In other words, remember that those you tread on, on your way up the ladder of success, you will have to deal with on the way back down.

Destiny dates

Positive: 1, 2, 3, 4, 5, 6, 17, 18, 19, 20, 21, 22, 24, 25, 26, 27, 28, 29

Negative: 30, 31

Mixed: 7, 8, 9, 10, 11, 12, 13, 14, 15, 16, 23

Highlights of the month

You're all hyped up and wired up by Mercury in June. Curb your speech a little to avoid misunderstandings and arguments, especially after the 5th when Jupiter enters the twelfth zone of your horoscope. You may be excessive and say the wrong thing to the wrong person. Timing is everything at this time.

With Jupiter's entry into this twelfth zone, your compassionate nature also grows. There's a distinct humanitarian flavour to this aspect and it could plug you in to all sorts of new opportunities to improve the lives of those who are disadvantaged and less happy or successful than yourself.

After the 6th, Venus produces a favourable aspect to your career, as does Jupiter, indicating additional means of income and opportunities for the taking. There's nothing stopping you at this time, when Venus radiates your personality with its entry into your Sun sign after the 10th. Be careful of those who may be jealous of your success. It's best not to advertise all of your wins and joys too readily until you test the waters with others first.

This is a month where your friendships can bedazzle you and your creative power is at a peak. Between the 13th and 18th you'll experience the benefits of Venus and Mars in your horoscope. Venus in its aspect to Uranus uplifts you in the company of friends and attracts you to those who are not in your normal clique or circle. You will expand your understanding and meet with those who have different views on life. You will like the variety of colours that are casting hues over your experiences now, and the presence of Mars also means there is some additional energy around to make that happen. Your motto at this time will be 'life is not a spectator sport'.

Take up some sort of new art form or hobby that will do you the world of good between the 19th and 21st. Painting, music or even some form of dance could bring out that hidden or latent talent that you have yet to share with the world. Explore these avenues of self-expression to the fullest extent, because you will be completely satisfied by doing so.

Care should be taken after the 22nd, when Mars activates your Sun sign. Impulsiveness, rash behaviour and speed are all sources of danger to you. You must slow everything down and, if you are driving or using machinery, pay extra attention to what you are doing. The 23rd is also particularly important inasmuch as Mars and Neptune create some sort of reaction to environmental factors such as pharmaceuticals and/or alcohol. Pay special attention to your diet and other medicinal compounds that may not agree with you.

Between the 24th and 30th, Venus and Mars again bring you energy, dynamic interactions and attractive alliances. These last few days of June will certainly bring a smile to your face.

Romance and friendship

Your sense of humour is excellent between the 1st and the 6th. Your quick wit will win you a few new friends, so don't be afraid to tell a joke, relate a story or use your powers of persuasion to get what you want.

You are quite amorous between the 9th and the 11th, but may put too much energy into one relationship to the exclusion of everything else. Be conscious of the needs of all of your friends at this time, otherwise some of your mates could get their noses out of joint.

You need to repay someone a debt of gratitude between the 12th and the 14th. Don't postpone this because you could come across as being selfish, only wanting the help of others when you need them. Reciprocate. Generously open your heart and give. This is an excellent way to grow your love and friendships.

The 15th until the 18th is a romantic and lustful period. Your sensuality peaks. Take advantage of it!

Watch your health, your words and activities between the 17th and the 22nd. Mars's impact on your Sun sign causes you to run headlong into problems without thinking. Use this energy constructively to build bridges, not destroy them.

The Moon in your zone of friendship after the 23rd makes for fun times. Mixing with those of like mind will bring you great pleasure. A secret rendezvous around the 26th is highlighted and will probably be exciting but not long lasting.

Don't overreact to the words of someone around the 28th. On the 29th, as well, you are reactive and need to get your feelings under control. Things smooth out for you by the 30th.

Work and money

You have to remodel yourself from time to time and June is one such period. The solar eclipse on the 2nd indicates a release of a whole lot of latent energies within you. Direct these energies carefully, even if at first you feel a little bit confused about how you can take advantage of the power within you.

Monetary outgoings could push you to your limits as Jupiter moves to your zone of expenses on the 4th. This effect occurs over a long-term period, so there's no point sweeping these issues under the rug to avoid them. Take the bull by the horns, assume the responsibility for your actions and become controlled about your financial policy.

Domestic and residential property is spotlighted between the 8th and the 12th. Either spending money to beautify your home or possibly investing in a real estate transaction is worthwhile pursuing.

Partnerships are highlighted after the 14th, especially around the 16th during the lunar eclipse. The hidden characteristics of someone may cause you to doubt the effectiveness of the relationship. Think again. From the 21st till the 23rd your profits and your self-esteem expand.

An argument on the 29th paves the way for some positive results because you're able to clear the air with someone who's been obstructing you.

Destiny dates

Positive: 1, 3, 6, 8, 9, 10, 11, 15, 16, 24, 25, 26, 27, 30

Negative: 23

Mixed: 2, 4, 5, 12, 13, 14, 17, 18, 19, 20, 21, 22, 28, 29

Highlights of the month

Eliminate what's unnecessary in your life this month, even if you desperately want to hang on to it. With Mars moving through your Sun sign, you may become aggressive if you feel thwarted in your desire for something. From the 4th, Venus accentuates your love of luxury, pleasure and spending, which could be a problem, especially if you're answerable to someone else about how the money is being used.

By the 6th you'll feel confident you can curb your impulses and spend wisely on whatever it is that is necessary. With items that are not really important, you'll be more able to defer the impulse to buy them until a later date.

You'll be feeling warm and fuzzy in your relationships after the 9th because Venus and Jupiter lend you emotional support. You will, however, experience a few small glitches in your communications and intimacy between the 13th and 19th. At this time it is probably better to spend time alone rather than forcing the hand of someone who is not as amenable to your advances as you would like them to be.

Relationships again pick up steam around the 25th, and this is also an appropriate time to use your skills and positive personality traits to make inroads into your professional future.

However, around the 28th, Mars, the combative planet that could be the source of a few problems this month, also rears its head in your workplace. The competitiveness with your peers might distract you from getting your work done. Trivial matters should be discarded and addressed at a later time.

You will also need to set an example to others throughout this contentious period. Being on your best behaviour will impress those who can assist you in your professional activities. However, any favouritism shown to you by someone above may only serve to create more friction between you and another person, who feels you are being singled out for special treatment. You'll need to balance your loyalties very carefully at this time.

Venus transiting in the third zone of travels, contracts and other communications on the 29th favours any sort of agreements that you need to execute. Rest assured that the soft vibrations of this planet mean you won't have to be too ruthless in your negotiations. In fact, a more cordial approach will win you favours and cut you a better deal in the long run.

Romance and friendship

On the 1st, being honest will not necessarily win you any accolades. Someone in your family may feel as if you're being harsh. You'll probably end up regretting being so transparent because the displeasure others exhibit is based upon their perception of you being callous in your opinion. You need to call a spade a spade, and leave it at that.

Communications improve between the 2nd and the 5th. Burying the hatchet is the name of the game, particularly if you've had any sort of long-standing negative feelings towards someone. Perhaps they've acted improperly and you've spoken your piece. Now is the time to let bygones be bygones and move on to a new cycle with them.

Your imagination is wild and exuberant after the 8th. You mustn't let anyone discourage your hopes or dreams.

You are trying to cram too much social life into the small amount of time you have available between the 11th and the 16th. Perhaps you fear that people will forget you? Or that you'll cease being the flavour of the month? All this serves to prove that perhaps during this small cycle, the planets are causing you to have some self-doubts.

Karma will, however, deal you a much better hand between the 18th and the 21st. Are you prepared to take what it has to offer? You mustn't allow fear to dominate your decisions to foster better relationships, even if what occurs is something of an unknown factor.

The wildcard, if you could call it that, will bring you some satisfaction now.

When Mercury enters your zone of personal comfort and security on the 29th, you'll be focusing much more on what you can do to gain some assurances from your family.

Work and money

I must caution you not to dive headlong into some sort of job or workplace scenario that you haven't given enough thought to. Between the 1st and the 4th spend a little time researching what probably seems like an opportunity too good to be true. It probably is.

Don't have too many high expectations between the 5th and the 10th. You're probably all fired up about changing your routine, getting the thumbs up from your co-workers, only to find that they feel a little threatened by these unexpected manoeuvres on your part. Consultation is your key word.

Opportunities abound from the 16th up until the 21st. You'll be in your element at this time and can draw upon your extensive knowledge to improve your income and good standing with others. Education and muted bits of information that you've acquired will come in handy at this time.

From the 24th till the 30th, a touch of impatience will be based upon your hard work not giving you the results you'd like to see as quickly as possible.

All I can say, Gemini, is that you need to be a little more patient.

Destiny dates

Positive: 20, 21

Negative: 11, 12

Mixed: 1, 2, 3, 4, 5, 6, 7, 8, 9, 10, 13, 14, 15, 16, 17, 18, 19, 24, 25, 26, 27, 28, 29, 30

Highlights of the month

If you've planned to develop a more independent path throughout 2011, the period of the 3rd to the 5th is a perfect time to seek out financial backing for your concepts. There are great developments apparent in your career and you can look forward to laying down the foundations for your ambitions. Anyone who is in a position to assist you financially should be spoken to now and you should also take special care with your business plan and mission statements.

Even if you're not particularly partial to business as such, it's not a bad idea to look at where you are and where you would like to be in future. Once you've planned and visualised what it is you want, it's amazing just how much easier it is to get from A to B.

You're still determined to earn money and do whatever needs to be done to get ahead; however, don't let arguments drain you of valuable energy.

Your values and standards may still be differing from those of a significant other and you need to compromise in some way.

After the 6th, a friend may require help. The compassionate side of your nature will come to the forefront and is strongly highlighted during this period. This will make you feel good because Venus gives you the ability to extend your hand in friendship and generosity.

Around the 8th make sure you are on the right side of the tracks, morally speaking. Compromising your standards is possible at this time, and you don't want to be left feeling indebted morally or ethically. Just remind yourself of the consequences of your actions and the repercussions not only on yourself but on others in the future.

You'll be wondering if there is a sequel to some outing or event you have enjoyed with someone. This could be a romantic interlude you are wishing will continue, but the person you are interested in may have become conspicuously absent, causing you to feel some sort of emotional frustration.

By the 26th you could find yourself back-pedalling and filling your mind with contradictory images of what could have, should have, would have been, etc. You must overcome this obsessive behaviour and not let Pluto overtake your sensibilities.

Your vision is back to 20–20 by the 30th, when Venus and Jupiter give you clarity on relationships and what it is you truly desire, or what is or isn't worthwhile pursuing. You need this to give you a sense of calm and positive momentum as you move into the coming month.

Romance and friendship

What goes around, comes around, as the old karmic saying goes, and from the 1st till the 3rd what you give will result in a proportionate amount of receiving on your part. Putting this into action could be difficult for you, particularly around the 4th, when the Moon is in close proximity to Saturn. Don't begrudge giving and, if you have to do it, do it with an open heart.

Watch your health between the 6th and the 8th. It's quite likely there's nothing wrong with you physically, but your emotions are having an impact on your physical wellbeing. Your nervous system is highly strung and therefore you need to find some new methods of bringing peace and calm to your mind. This in turn will of course have a resultant effect, a positive one, on your health and overall welfare.

You're in good company between the 15th and the 17th. The energies of the Sun, some of the karmic planets and Venus and Mercury, too, are all positive factors in the way you are able to connect very easily with others.

You're interested in trying new things, culturally expanding your horizons, and possibly even travelling somewhere. For some of you, after the 21st, an impulse to change house, move away for a while or just take some long service leave, could take hold. Trust your heart.

You have immense willpower around the 29th. What this means is that, if there are some lingering bad habits you've been trying to break, then now's the time to make the effort. For those of you who are finding it difficult, why not consider hypnosis or other meditation aids that can give you the strength to overcome some of these negative behaviours? They undermine your health over the long term.

Work and money

The passage of time can sometimes make you feel a little dry when it comes to work, especially if you've been doing the same thing over and over again for a long while. You need to freshen up again, and this requires you to reappraise your courses of action between the 1st and the 5th.

It will be time to upgrade your manifesto. Your biography and your resumé are both important, especially if you're looking to break new ground, get new work and improve your financial standing. If you haven't done this for a while and you're considering a meeting after the 8th, you could feel a little exposed. Be prepared.

Your sleep could be horrific if you're worrying about little things after the 17th. By the 20th this can improve but it may well have to do with a lack of exercise. You can improve your work skills simply by moving your body.

A professional alliance with someone may be paper thin. You haven't yet taken the time to look over the fence to consider if there's a Plan B. Don't proceed on any course of contractual association until you've perused your options. Many new things can come to light between the 25th and the 28th that could cause you to change your mind. This will be a good thing.

Your ideas need to be inclusive of others and their concepts between the 29th and the 31st. It's all about team effort at the end of August.

Destiny dates

Positive: 15, 16, 20, 21, 25, 27, 28, 29, 30, 31
Negative: 7
Mixed: 1, 2, 3, 4, 5, 6, 8, 17, 26

SEPTEMBER
2011

Highlights of the month

Acting in a superior way is not how to win friends around the 5th. Having self-confidence is very different to showing off or unconsciously using your ego to push others around. Conversely, it may not actually be you who is ill-behaved, but someone else you have to deal with at this time. You need to set up some boundaries, both for yourself and others. There may be cultural or customary differences between you and those you come in contact with during the first few days of the month. Try to study the situation before you get yourself in too deep. A little information can go a long way.

You have to be obliging in your workplace circumstances between the 12th and 19th. You may not like the way things are done but, fortunately, Mars in a favourable aspect to your zone of career gives you the ability to control your desires, employ some diplomacy in your speech and create a win–win situation.

You may have to burst the bubble of a friend who appears to be acting like a type of tragic Phoenix, flying above the world in some sort of illusory state over love. When what you have to say shatters their reality and reveals the truth to them about someone, they may initially take out their disappointment on you. Explain to them your reasons for stating the obvious, and I am sure they will understand your intentions are noble in every possible way.

This month Mars acts as a positive catalyst for many of your activities. A good work-out is an excellent method of decompressing the tensions around you. Getting healthy, reconsidering your diet and looking at other ways to improve your self-image will all be important this month. Together with the influence of Uranus, you're able to think outside the square and achieve these results with completely new and novel methods.

You'll find it increasingly easier to make new friends, but towards the end of the month don't let others lay a guilt trip on you if they are not in the same position as you are to enjoy their social lives and friendships. At best you can share some of your 'secrets' and hopefully they too will be able to experience the uplifting vibrations of some of the planets currently surrounding you, such as Venus, which is instrumental in enabling you to cement new friendships during this lucky phase of your life.

Around the 30th, Venus once again conjoins Saturn in your creative zone of relationships, children and love affairs. Sometimes it's hard to sit on the sidelines while children or other loved ones flounder. It's not impossible for you to help them get out of the rut they happen to be in, but you must under no circumstances shoulder the responsibility for all of the actions they need to execute to turn things around. Offer your advice, but that should be as far as it goes.

Romance and friendship

To keep growing emotionally you sometimes need to let go of things. On the 1st, 2nd and also the 6th, it's time for you to let go. You can't repackage the past into some format that you think is going to serve you now and in the future. Look carefully at the people you've been with and you'll realise, probably by the 8th or the 9th, that change is inevitable and you need to be adaptable to make relationships work. Otherwise, you do need to walk away.

You have an opportunity to shine between the 11th and the 13th. There's something about you at the moment—and even you may not be able to put your finger on it—which is electrifying and attractive to others. You have a new stance and are able to dump pretension. Honesty is part of your attractiveness now and will win you some favours. Sidestep any sort of controversy, particularly if it's gossip that's being handed down through the grapevine.

Between the 16th and the 21st it's best to remain unaffected by what others say, either about yourself or others. There may be the odd troll or two spring-ing up from nowhere, trying to sway your opinion with some sort of mechanical speech. You'll see through it.

If you're single, Mercury will spark an interest in a new flame between the 25th and the 28th. The planets at this stage give you full author-ity to explore possibilities and to press on with your search for diversity, which is your trademark. Interactive opportunities bring mental as well as physical stimulation.

A friend could be very reassuring to you around the 29th. If you're having problems with a lover or a friend, another mutual acquaintance may understand precisely where you're at on the 30th. Speaking to them, you'll sense they know exactly where you're coming from. Isn't compassion a wonderful thing?

Work and money

We are all consumers, there's no doubt about that. But from the 1st till the 6th you will find yourself consuming a little more than you'd intended to, thereby putting a little more pressure on your finances. You need to identify areas that are neces-sary expenditures, and those which aren't. You need to curtail some of your excessive spending habits in order to get ahead financially. Remember that if you look after the pennies, the dollars will look after themselves.

Time is in short supply between the 9th and the 15th. You need to sift out what's unimportant so you can finish the tasks that have been given to you. There could be open and unapologetic interruptions by co-workers. This could irritate you no end, which will see you getting mobile and out of the crossfire of endless chit-chat.

You're a person on a mission and great things can be achieved if you go it alone, particularly from the 23rd till the 28th. At this time, you'll be in a better position to drown out the background white noise without your work being affected.

On the 30th you may forget where you've hidden some money. But rest assured it's not lost, just placed somewhere even you haven't recalled. It will turn up sooner or later.

Destiny dates

Positive: 23, 24, 25, 26, 27, 28, 29

Negative: 3, 4, 5, 9, 10, 11, 12, 13, 14, 15, 16, 17, 18, 19, 20, 21

Mixed: 1, 2, 6, 30

Highlights of the month

During this month, at least in the first three or four days, you'll realise you've been exerting an awful lot of energy in areas that may not exactly be returning your investment. You must re-establish the need to spend quality time with someone you love so that your relationships can become more balanced.

Around the 8th, you must agree to disagree with someone in your family and, in a worst case scenario, may have to ask them to mind their own business.

Relationships take an interesting turn after the 9th, when Venus enters your sixth zone of service, daily routine and work. Help is also covered by this particular area of your horoscope and therefore we can't discount the fact you may have to spend some time looking after someone in your family, your partner or a close friend. Here is your opportunity to show your love and compassion and do so in a selfless manner.

I don't often speak about another type of special relationship we have, which is with pets; those helpless little creatures like dogs and cats who often become closer to us than some humans. During this cycle you may acquire a new pet, or appreciate your dog or cat much more than usual, and forge a closer bond with them. This is also the zone of health, so don't disregard any minor ailments that your pet may exhibit because over time, their small problems may become more serious. Prevention is better than cure.

Don't think for a minute that just because someone has free advice to offer that it is in any way quality content. Be polite in receiving what is offered after the 26th; but by the same token, don't jump the gun by acting on advice that hasn't been tested or thoroughly appraised first.

Religious views, the way you perceive yourself in relation to others and your overall life perception will change dramatically after the 29th. Jupiter along with Pluto will radically shift your attitudes to make you aware of bigger and better things. It's as if you have X-ray vision and can see beneath the surface of things and people. This could be rather surprising if not shocking when you start to sense elements of people's characters that may not have been evident before. You'll know precisely how to act, so remain open and let your heart determine which path you will now take.

Working collaboratively around the 30th will be fun and educational as well. Don't worry about whose bright idea it was in the first place. Even if there are others who want to take full credit for the job, remember that your strength and success lies in the enjoyment and creative output you experience during the process itself.

Romance and friendship

Life can seem like an endless train, especially when you're in the company of boring people. You may want bigger and better things in your social life, especially from the 2nd till the 6th, so go for it and enjoy this new phase.

A recent omission on your part may have someone sulking and you don't know why. You're confused over love between the 8th and the 10th and need to backtrack over your discussions carefully to see where you may have inadvertently offended them. It's probably nothing big but they are overreacting.

Sometimes it's not money that we're robbed of—in life the odd passing thief can take our emotions and our wellbeing as well. Around the 13th be careful of strangers you meet who may spin a wonderful yarn but who are really ultimately only looking to feather their own nests. Don't be too quick to give your heart so readily to someone.

Greater responsibilities from the 14th till the 22nd mean that you may not have the time you'd like to spend with others. Carefully assess which people deserve your time and love.

You need to be diverse in your sympathy on the 28th and the 29th. You may be surprised to find that several friends or family members simultaneously need your help. This could be a challenge but at the same time you'll enjoy offering your advice and sharing your wisdom and secret methods of dealing with life's problems.

On the 30th, be careful that Mercury and Mars don't cause you to be a little too hot-headed in your desire to help someone. It could backfire and cause an argument.

Work and money

You're only as big as your last hit, as the recording industry says. Continuing to demand a position of high virtue will sometimes hold no weight with others, particularly if you're looking to achieve a better position, a more secure financial arrangement, or honour and respect in your work. You need to come up with something fresh, alive and creatively competitive between the 2nd and the 5th.

Independently employed Geminis should take care from the 9th because Venus, entering the zone of debt, shows that you may lavish unnecessary objects, services and expenses on your business only to find yourself incapable of paying for them on time. Get some professional assistance and additional management skills to help tide you over.

Between the 15th and the 24th you need to enter into contracts by assuming a position of least liability. There is a favourite acronym of very wealthy people and that is to use 'OPM', meaning 'Other People's Money'. Don't make yourself liable when you don't have any guarantees.

Jupiter and Pluto conclude the month with some powerful energy that indicates the need to balance what you and others are sharing in the way of costs and savings.

Destiny dates

Positive: 2, 3, 4, 5, 6, 23, 24
Negative: 8, 10, 13, 26
Mixed: 9, 14, 15, 16, 17, 18, 19, 20, 21, 22, 28, 29, 30

Highlights of the month

Don't be taken in by sweet words and other fake gestures on the 1st. You may be feeling vulnerable, desirous of love and affection, only to find yourself overlooking some of the frailties and even deceptions of another. However, with Venus moving into your zone of marriage and partnerships on the 2nd, try not to throw out the baby with the bathwater. You need to sift the genuine from the fake, the wheat from the chaff; those who would hoodwink you from those who genuinely have your best interests at heart.

Sudden meetings, falling in love at first sight and experiencing exciting social changes are all part of the mix throughout November, especially after the 3rd. Explore different venues and of course don't forget that these days it's as simple as going onto the Internet and searching for what's available and fun around town. This is an excellent way to meet new friends through different social networking and dating sites.

From around the 11th, your home affairs once again take precedence over everything else. You need to look carefully at how you can spend quality time with some family members. This might be a joint decision you need to discuss with your partner about how much time they want to spend with your family, and vice versa. Once again, keep the lines of communication open.

You are keen and generous after the 17th, but be warned that your receptiveness may make friends become a little too demanding of you, especially if you are in a new relationship that is fresh and time consuming. You need to watch out for jealousy and clearly demarcate the boundaries over which no one should step. This might seem a little severe at first, but once you dictate the terms, it's quite likely the relationship will flow very smoothly.

You have incredible determination and will-power this month, and the period leading up to the 25th reflects this very strongly. Even if time is putting a huge amount of strain on you, you'll be able to keep up and surprise others with your endurance and high levels of energy.

You could unknowingly be putting others under pressure during this cycle, so take stock of your situation and how well people are able to adjust to your changing schedules and demands. If others seem a little bit down and out around you, it could be that they feel you are being somewhat insensitive to their needs and the pace at which they can move. Slow things down a little and you will still be able to maintain your intensity without racing to the finish line. This will give everyone a chance to enjoy the journey with you.

Romance and friendship

Your or someone else's tears are distorted on the 1st. The pain you're experiencing is really not so bad and is just being amplified by your severe concerns. By the 2nd you'll realise that things are actually nowhere near as bad as you first thought.

Mars entering the fourth house on the 11th sets off alarm bells, astrologically speaking. Stay away from people whom you know full well are only out to have a fight and accuse you of something you're not guilty of. Discard any kind of ball and chain from the 14th to the 17th if you feel as though you're being held down under someone's thumb.

The Sun, in its hard aspect to Neptune, shows a few confronting self-issues around the 21st. The answer to these sorts of inner dilemmas is always spiritual. Use your intuition, listen to that still voice inside to make your decisions and to break through into clarity.

The period of the 22nd to the 24th is a wonderful phase for elevating yourself to a state of great popularity. Your flashing aura should be employed to win hearts. You may, however, incur the wrath of some do-goody philosopher who thinks that you should be more prim and proper in the way you approach matters.

A solar eclipse on the 25th also has much to say about your significant relationships, such as marriage. Between the 26th and the 28th your partner or lover seems distant. It could be that you're projecting some fear onto their reaction. It may well be that they are having trouble in their own personal lives, and can't easily tell you what's going on with them at the moment. You may assume that you're the problem, which is not the case. Give them space and this too will blow over.

You'll be assessing your romantic antics from the wrong position from the 29th to the 30th. You've only got your own self to blame if your behaviour causes a romance to come to zilch. Two of your important key words at the end of November are temperance and circumspection.

Work and money

There's nothing holding you back from achieving anything that you wish to achieve in November; however, on the 1st and the 2nd you could feel a little confused about what your life's mission is. Wait till the 3rd or 4th, when Mercury gives you much greater clarity and the ability to extract some vital information from others who hold the keys.

It's what's not said that is going to be important for you in your work between the 10th and the 14th. Read between the lines; use your silence as a weapon for gaining the upper hand in some negotiation.

Mars and Jupiter give you an extraordinary abundance of energy and ability on the 16th and the 17th. Things will be moving fast, so don't get carried away in the emotion of the moment. When it comes to business and money, think twice before signing away your life.

You'll have some unexpected shifts in your work between the 26th and the 30th. You're emotional about what you do, and also in your responses to those who may have opinions about the way you're doing your work or the amount of time it's taking. Keep a level head and also don't forget to give credit to others where it is due.

Destiny dates

Positive: 3, 12, 13, 14, 16, 17, 22, 23, 24
Negative: 5, 6, 7, 8, 9, 21
Mixed: 1, 2, 4, 10, 11, 25, 26, 27, 28, 29, 30

DECEMBER 2011

Highlights of the month

At the close of the year, during December, remain flexible, even if you feel impelled to maintain your ideals. You have to slash through constraints this month and between the 1st and 6th you have the ability to do so. However, maintain your cool under pressure because you don't want to get others offside, especially knowing that people's tempers flare up much more readily just before Christmas.

Venus and Pluto mean that your love can be intense and you can rekindle old flames of passion during this final period of 2011.

Your presence will be required at a party after the 7th and you have the ability to fulfil some of your passionate desires. The unfortunate thing is, however, that you can't duplicate yourself and be in two places at once. You may have to sacrifice something for the sake of being at a function you prefer.

You have a frantic thirst for knowledge and achievement and could find yourself racing against the clock leading up to the 17th. You need to plan your work and not fall into the dangerous terrain of management by terror. If you remember to organise your diary in the early part of December, you can and will be able to manage all of the demands placed on you during this last month of the year.

Venus enters into the favourable ninth zone of your horoscope around the 21st, indicating travels and pleasant Christmas events. Get your shopping done early and, even if you only have occasional contact with people, make it a point to extend your hand in friendship to them at least at Christmas.

I can make a fairly liberal prediction and say that the last few days of 2011 should be a mixture of great joy and some exciting tension. Around the 22nd, you may be slightly disappointed that someone cancels their engagement with you. But if you think about it, this will serve to give you additional time to do some of the more pressing things. You can always catch up with them at a later stage.

On the 24th someone may regard you as an experienced shoulder to cry on. Don't respond with rash logic because this may not satisfy their particular need. You have to appraise carefully what is bothering them and, if you are unable to be completely honest with them for fear of hurting them more, just calm them and help them to collect themselves until they are in a better position to appreciate what you have to relate.

One of the final main aspects of the year is Venus influencing your Sun sign on the 30th. This should give you an excellent sense of completion, self-worth and social connectivity. Certainly this is a wonderful way to finish 2011.

Romance and friendship

Don't let carelessness wound the feelings of someone between the 2nd and the 5th. You need to be sensitive to people's needs just now. Christmas is approaching and the hustle and bustle of life could make it easy for you to run roughshod over others' feelings. Pay more attention to where they might be coming from.

Venus and Mars are excellent for your love life from the 6th till the 10th, which could be rich and fulfilling, but there could be some acute problems in your neighbourhood or with a sibling. This could be almost like a roller-coaster period that requires constant improvement day by day on your part.

You probably feel as if you need a helpful magic spell to bring someone under control around the 15th. Feeling as though your extra efforts, attempts and words are falling on deaf ears, you'll possibly decide to give up and look elsewhere, where you feel the grass is greener.

Changes are afoot with troubles definitely on the cards after the 19th. With Venus entering your zone of long-distance travels on the 21st, this is an excellent time either to pack your suitcases and leave, or at least get out your travel brochures and effectively plan what you're going to do over Christmas and the new year. Incidentally, make sure you choose the right sort of companion to do this with!

The three days leading up to Christmas, from the 22nd till the 25th, will be rather intense but it's up to you to remain neutral in a situation that requires at least one person to remain calm. You're competent to do so and, by getting through this final tense social situation, you'll feel on top of the world as Christmas 2011 comes around.

The year 2011 may well be ending, but with this optimistic energy welling up from within you, you'll feel as if it's just the beginning again.

Work and money

Travelling is extremely productive in the final month of the year and you need to cough up a few extra dollars if you are going to do this properly. An investment just now to travel outside your normal locality will yield good results, especially if you're in sales, marketing or acting as an agent for someone else. From the 1st until the 6th, you'll be extremely busy, but from the 7th, you may finally land a deal that has been long awaited.

Mars is in conflict with some of your cultural desires, and those in your environment may not be amenable to what you request between the 11th and the 15th. Fortunately, after the 14th, Mercury moves in its direct motion, allowing you to move forward in full control and armed with all the correct facts.

A last-minute burst of energy helps you achieve a great deal in the office or with a backlog of paperwork between the 19th and the 22nd. Don't postpone any of this because it will weigh heavily on your mind throughout the Christmas break. Get it done so that you can fully relax throughout this festive season and end 2011 on a wonderfully positive note.

Destiny dates

Positive: 21, 30
Negative: 8, 9, 10, 11, 12, 13, 14, 17, 19
Mixed: 1, 2, 3, 4, 5, 6, 7, 15, 22, 23, 24, 25

2011:
Astronumerology

I saw the angel in the marble and carved until i set him free

—Michaelangelo

The power behind your name

It's hard to believe that your name resonates with a numerical vibration, but it's true! By simply adding the numbers of your name, you can see which planet rules you and what effects your name will have on your life and destiny. According to the ancient Chaldean system of numerology, each number is assigned a planetary energy. Take a look at the chart below to see how each alphabetical letter is connected to a planetary energy:

AIQJY	=	1	Sun
BKR	=	2	Moon
CGLS	=	3	Jupiter
DMT	=	4	Uranus
EHNX	=	5	Mercury
UVW	=	6	Venus
OZ	=	7	Neptune
FP	=	8	Saturn
—	=	9	Mars

The number 9 is not allotted a letter because it is considered 'unknowable'. Once the numbers have been added, establish which single planet rules your name and personal affairs. At this point the number 9 can be used for interpretation. Do you think it's unusual that many famous actors, writers and musicians have modified their names? This is to attract luck and good fortune, which can be made easier by using the energies of a friendlier planet. Try experimenting with the table and see how new names affect you. It's so much fun, and you may even attract greater love, wealth and worldly success!

Look at the following example to work out the power of your name. A person named Andrew Brown would calculate his ruling planet by correlating each letter to a number in the table, like this:

A	N	D	R	E	W	B	R	O	W	N
1	5	4	2	5	6	2	2	7	6	5

Now add the numbers like this:

$$1 + 5 + 4 + 2 + 5 + 6 + 2 + 2 + 7 + 6 + 5 = 45$$

$$\text{Then add } 4 + 5 = 9$$

The ruling number of Andrew Brown's name is 9, which is ruled by Mars (see how the 9 can now be used?). Now study the name–number table to reveal the power of your name. The numbers 4 and 5 will also play a secondary role in Andrew's character and destiny, so in this case you would also study the effects of Uranus (4) and Mercury (5).

Name–number table

Your name-number	Ruling planet	Your name characteristics
1	Sun	Attractive personality. Magnetic charm. Superman-, superwoman-like vitality and physical energy. Incredibly active and gregarious. Enjoys outdoor activities and sports. Has friends and individuals in powerful positions. Good government connections. Intelligent, spectacular, flashy and successful. A loyal number for love and relationships.
2	Moon	Feminine and soft, emotional temperament. Fluctuating moods but intuitive, and possibly even clairvoyant abilities. Ingenious nature and kind-hearted expression of feelings. Loves family, mothering and home life. Night owl who probably needs more sleep. Success with the public and/or women generally.
3	Jupiter	Sociable, optimistic number with fortunate destiny. Attracts opportunities without too much effort. Great sense of timing. Religious or spiritual inclinations. Naturally drawn to investigate the meaning of life. Philosophical insight. Enjoys travel and to explore the world and different cultures.
4	Uranus	Volatile character with many peculiar aspects. Likes to experiment and test novel experiences. Forward thinking, with many extraordinary friends. Gets bored easily so needs plenty of inspiring activities. Pioneering, technological and creative. Wilful and obstinate at times. Unforeseen events in life may be positive or negative.

Your name-number	Ruling planet	Your name characteristics
5	Mercury	Sharp wit, quick thinking and with great powers of speech. Extremely active life. Always on the go, living on nervous energy. Youthful outlook and never grows old. Looks younger than actual age. Young friends and humorous disposition. Loves reading and writing. Great communicator.
6	Venus	Delightful and charming. Graceful and eye-catching personality who cherishes and nourishes friends. Very active social life. Musical or creative interests. Great moneymaking opportunities as well as numerous love affairs indicated. Career in the public eye is quite likely. Loves family but is often troubled over divided loyalties with friends.
7	Neptune	Intuitive, spiritual and self-sacrificing nature. Easily duped by those who need help. Loves to dream of life's possibilities. Has healing powers. Dreams are revealing and prophetic. Loves water and will have many journeys in life. Spiritual aspirations dominate worldly desires.
8	Saturn	Hard-working, ambitious person with slow yet certain achievements. Remarkable concentration and self-sacrifice for a chosen objective. Financially focused but generous when a person's trust is gained. Proficient in one's chosen field but is a hard taskmaster. Demands perfection and needs to relax and enjoy life.

Your name-number	Ruling planet	Your name characteristics
9	Mars	Extraordinary physical drive, desires and ambition. Sports and outdoor activities are major keys to health. Confrontational but likes to work and play really hard. Protects and defends family, friends and territory. Individual tastes in life but also self-absorbed. Needs to listen to others' advice to gain greater successes.

Your 2011 planetary ruler

Astrology and numerology are intimately connected. As already shown, each planet rules over a number between 1 and 9. Both your name and your birth date are governed by planetary energies.

Simply add the numbers of your birth date and the year in question to find out which planet will control the coming year for you. Here is an example:

If you were born on the 12th of November, add the numerals 1 and 2, for your day of birth, and 1 and 1, for your month of birth, to the year in question, in this case 2011, the current year, like this:

Add 1 + 2 + 1 + 1 + 2 + 0 + 1+ 1 = 9

The planet ruling your individual karma for 2011 will be Mars because this planet rules the number 9.

You can even take your ruling name-number, as shown previously, and add it to the year in question, to throw more light on your coming personal affairs, like this:

A N D R E W B R O W N = 9
Year coming = 2011
Add 9 + 2 + 0 + 1 + 1 = 13
Add 1 + 3 = 4

This is the ruling year number, using your name-number as a basis.

Therefore, study Uranus's (number 4) influence for 2011. Enjoy!

1 is the year of the Sun

Overview

The year 2011 is the commencement of a new cycle for you. Because the Sun rules the number 1, the dominant energy for you in the coming year is solar, which is also connected to the sign of Leo. Expect the coming year to be full of great accomplishments and a high reputation regarding new plans and projects. This is the turning of a new page in the book of your life.

You will experience an uplifting of your physical energies, which makes you ready to assume fresh responsibilities in a new nine-year cycle. Whatever you begin now will surely be successful.

Your physical vitality is strong and your health should improve. If you've been suffering physical ailments, this is the time to improve your physical wellbeing because recovery will be certain.

You're a magnetic person this year, so attracting people into your life won't be difficult. Expect a new circle of friends and possibly even new lovers coming into your life. Get ready to be invited to many parties and different engagements. However, don't go burning the midnight oil because this will overstretch your physical powers.

Don't be too cocky with friends or employers. Maintain some humility, which will make you even more popular throughout 2011.

Love and pleasure

Because this is the commencement of a new cycle, you'll be lucky in love. The Sun also has influence over children, so your family life will also entail more responsibility. Music, art and any other creative activities will be high on your agenda and may be the source of a new romance for you.

Work

Because you are so popular and powerful this year, you won't need to exert too much effort to attract luck, money and new windows of opportunity through your work and group activities. Changes that you make professionally now will pay off, particularly in the coming couple of years. Promotions are likely and don't be surprised to see some extra money coming your way as a pay rise.

Improving your luck

Because Leo and the number 1 are your rulers this year, you'll be especially lucky without too much effort. The months of July and August, being ruled by Leo, are very lucky for you. The 1st, 8th, 15th and 22nd hours of Sundays will be especially lucky. You may also find yourself meeting Leos and they may be able to contribute something to your good fortune throughout the coming year.

This year your lucky numbers are 1, 10, 19 and 28.

2 is the year of the Moon

Overview

The Moon represents emotional, nurturing, mothering and feminine aspects of our natures and 2011 will embody all of these traits in you, and more.

Groundbreaking opportunities in your relationships with family members can be expected. This will offer you immense satisfaction.

Your emotional and mental moods and habits should be examined. If you are reactive in your life, this year will be the perfect time to take greater control of yourself. The sign of Cancer, which is ruled by the Moon, is also very much linked to the number 2 and therefore people born under this sign may have an important role to play in your life.

Love and pleasure

Your home, family life and interpersonal relationships will be the main arenas of activity for you in 2011. You'll be able to take your relationships to a new level. If you haven't had the time to dedicate and devote yourself to the people you love, you can do so throughout the coming twelve months.

Thinking of moving? These lunar energies may cause you to change your residence or renovate your current home to make your living circumstances much more in tune with your mind and your heart.

Work

Working from home can be a great idea—or at least, spending more time alone to focus your attention on what you really want—will benefit you professionally. You need to control yourself and think carefully about how you are going to achieve your desired goals.

Women can be a source of opportunity for you and, if you're looking for a change in work, use your connections, especially feminine ones, to achieve success.

Improving your luck

The sign of Cancer being ruled by the Moon also has a connection with Mondays and therefore this will be one of your luckier days throughout 2011. The month of July is also one in which some of your dreams may come true. The 1st, 8th, 15th and 22nd hours on Mondays are successful times. Pay special attention to the new and full Moons in 2011.

The numbers 2, 11, 20, 29 and 38 are lucky for you.

3 is the year of Jupiter

Overview

Number 3 is one of the luckiest numbers, being

ruled by Jupiter. Therefore, 2011 should be an exciting and expansive year for you. The planet Jupiter and the sign of Sagittarius will dominate the affairs of your life.

Under the number 3 you'll desire a richer, deeper and broader experience of life and as a result your horizons will also be much broader. You have the ability to gain money, to increase your popularity, and to have loads of fun.

Generosity is one of the key words of the number 3 and you're likely to help others fulfil their desires, too. There is an element of humanity and self-sacrifice indicated by this number and so the more spiritual and compassionate elements of your personality will bubble to the surface. You can improve yourself as a person generally, and this is also a year when your good karma should be used unselfishly to help others as well as yourself.

Love and pleasure

Exploring the world through travel will be an important component of your social and romantic life throughout 2011. It's quite likely that, through your travels and your contacts in other places, you may meet people who will spur you on to love and romance.

You'll be a bit of a gambler in 2011 and the number 3 will make you speculative. This could mean a few false starts in the area of love, but don't be afraid to explore the signs of human possibilities. You may just meet your soulmate as a result.

If you're currently in a relationship, you can deepen your love for each other and push the relationship to new heights.

Work

This is a fortunate year for you. The year 2011 brings you opportunities and success. Your employers will listen to your ideas and accommodate your requests for extra money.

Starting a new job is likely, possibly even your own business. You will try something big and bold. Have no fear: success is on your side.

Improving your luck

As long as you don't push yourself too hard you will have a successful year. Maintain a first-class plan and stick to it. Be realistic about what you are capable of. On the 1st, 8th, 15th and 24th hours of Thursdays, your intuition will make you lucky.

Your lucky numbers this year are 3, 12, 21 and 30. March and December are lucky months. The year 2011 will bring you some unexpected surprises.

4 is the year of Uranus

Overview

Expect the unexpected in 2011. This is a year when you achieve extraordinary things but have to make serious choices between several opportunities. You need to break free of your own past self-limitations, off-load any baggage that is hindering you, in both your personal and professional lives.

It's an independent year and self-development will be important to achieving success.

Discipline is one of your key words for 2011. Maintain an orderly lifestyle, a clear-cut routine, and get more sleep. You'll gain strong momentum to fulfil yourself in each and every department of your life.

Love and pleasure

You may be dissatisfied with the current status quo in your relationships, so you're likely to break free and experiment with something different. Your relationships will be anything but dull or routine. You're looking for someone who is prepared to explore emotional and sexual landscapes.

Your social life will also be exciting and you'll meet unusual people who will open your eyes to new and fruitful activities. Spiritual and self-help activities will also capture your attention and enable you to make the most of your new friendships.

Work

The number 4 is modern, progressive and ruled by Uranus. Due to this, all sorts of technological gadgets, computing and Internet activities will play a significant role in your professional life. Move ahead with the times and upgrade your professional skills, because any new job you attempt will require it.

Work could be a little overwhelming, especially if you've not been accustomed to keeping a tight schedule. Be more efficient with your time.

Groups are important to your work efforts this year, so utilise your friends in finding a position you desire. Listen to their advice and become more of a team player because this will be a short cut in your pathway to success.

Improving your luck

Slow your pace this year because being impulsive will only cause you to make errors and waste time. 'Patience is a virtue', but in your case, when being ruled by the number 4, patience will be even more important for you.

The 1st, 8th, 15th and 20th hours of any Saturday will be very lucky for you in 2011.

Your lucky numbers are 4, 13, 22 and 31.

5 is the year of Mercury

Overview

Owing to the rulership of 2011 by the number 5, your intellectual and communicative abilities will be at a peak. Your imagination is also greatly stimulated by Mercury and so exciting new ideas will be constantly churning in your mind.

The downside of the number 5 is its convertible nature, which means it's likely that, when crunch times come and you have to make decisions, it will be difficult to do so. Get all your information together before drawing a firm conclusion. Develop a strong will and unshakable attitude to overcome distractions.

Contracts, new job offers and other agreements also need to be studied carefully before coming to any decision. Business skills and communication are the key words for your life in 2011.

Love and pleasure

One of the contributing factors to your love life in 2011 is service. You must learn to give to your partner if you wish to receive. There may be a change in your routine and this will be necessary if you are to keep your love life exciting, fresh and alive.

You could be critical, so be careful if you are trying to correct the behaviour of others. You'll be blunt and this will alienate you from your peers. Maintain some control over your critical mind before handing out your opinions.

You are likely to become interested in beautifying yourself and looking your best.

Work

Your ideas will be at the forefront of your professional activities this year. You are fast, capable and also innovative in the way you conduct yourself in the workplace. If you need to make any serious changes, however, it is best to think twice before 'jumping out of the pan and into the fire'.

Travel will also be a big component of your working life this year, and you can expect a hectic schedule with lots of flitting about here, there and everywhere. Pace yourself.

Improving your luck

Your greatest fortune will be in communicating ideas. Don't jump from one idea to another too quickly, though, because this will dilute your success.

Listen to your body signals as well because your health is strongly governed by the number 5. Sleep well, eat sensibly and exercise regularly to rebuild your resilience and strength.

The 1st, 8th, 15th and 20th hours of Wednesdays are your luckiest, so schedule your meetings and other important social engagements at these times.

Throughout 2011 your lucky numbers are 5, 14, 23 and 32.

6 is the year of Venus

Overview

The number 6 can be summed up in one beautiful four-letter word: LOVE! Venus rules 6 and is well known for its sensual, romantic and marital overtones. The year 2011 offers you all of this and more. If you're looking for a soulmate, it's likely to happen under a 6 vibration.

This year is a period of hard work to improve your security and finances. Saving money, cutting costs and looking to your future will be important. Keep in mind that this is a year of sharing love *and* material resources.

Love and pleasure

Romance is a key feature of 2011 and, if you're currently in a relationship, you can expect it to become more fulfilling. Important karmic connections are likely during this 6 year for those of you who are not yet married or in a relationship.

Beautify yourself, get a new hairstyle, work on looking your best through improving your fashion sense, new styles of jewellery and getting out there and showing the world what you're made of. This is a year in which your social engagements result in better relationships.

Try not to overdo it, because Venus has a tendency towards excess. Moderation in all things is important in a Venus year 6.

Work

The year 2011 will stimulate your knowledge about finance and your future security. You'll be capable of cutting back expenses and learning how to stretch a dollar. There could be surplus cash this year, increased income or some additional bonuses. You'll use this money to improve your living circumstances because home life is also important under a 6 year.

Your domestic situation could also be tied in with your work. During this year of Venus, your business and social activities will overlap.

Improving your luck

Money will flow as long as you keep an open mind and positive attitude. Remove negative personality traits obstructing you from greater luck. Be moderate in your actions and don't focus primarily on money. Your spiritual needs also require attention.

The 1st, 8th, 15th and 20th hours on Fridays are extremely lucky for you this year and new opportunities can arise when you least expect it.

The numbers 6, 15, 24 and 33 will generally increase your luck.

7 is the year of Neptune

Overview

Under a 7 year of Neptune, your spiritual and intuitive powers peak. Although your ideals seem clearer and more spiritually orientated, others may not understand your purpose. Develop the power of your convictions to balance your inner ideals with the practical demands of life.

You must learn to let go of your past emotional issues, break through these barriers to improve your life and your relationships this year. This might require you to sever ties with some of the usual people you have become accustomed to being with, which will give you the chance to focus on your own inner needs.

Love and pleasure

Relationships may be demanding and it's at this point in your life that you'll realise you have to give something to yourself as well, not just give to others indefinitely. If the people that matter most in your life are not reciprocating and meeting your needs, you'll have to make some important changes this year.

When it comes to helping others, pick your mark. Not everyone is deserving of the love and resources you have to offer. If you're indiscriminate, you could find yourself with egg on your face if you have been taken advantage of. Be firm, but compassionate.

Work

Compassionate work best describes 2011 under a 7 year. But the challenges of your professional life give you greater insight into yourself and the ability to see clearly what you *don't* want in your life any more. Remove what is unnecessary and this will pave the way for brighter successes.

Caring for and helping others will be important because your work will now bring you to a point where you realise that selfishness, money and security are not the only important things in life. Helping others will be part of your process, which will bring excellent benefits.

Improving your luck

Self-sacrifice, along with discipline and personal discrimination, bring luck. Don't let people use you because this will only result in more emotional baggage. The law of karma states that what you give, you will receive in greater measure; but sometimes the more you give, the more people take, too. Remember that.

The 1st, 8th, 15th and 20th hours of Tuesdays will be lucky times this year.

Try the numbers 7, 16, 25 and 34 to increase your luck.

8 is the year of Saturn

Overview

The number 8 is the most practical of the numbers, being ruled by Saturn and Capricorn. This means that your discipline, attention to detail and hard work will help you achieve your goals. Remaining solitary and not being overly involved with people will help you focus on things that matter. Resisting temptation will be part of your challenge this year, but doing so will also help you become a better person.

Love and pleasure

Balance your personal affairs with work. If you pay too much attention to your work, finances and your professional esteem, you may be missing out on the simple things in life, mainly love and affection.

Being responsible is certainly a great way to show your love to the ones who matter to you, such as your family members. But if you're concerned only with work and no play, it makes for a very dull family life. Make a little more time to enjoy your family and friends and schedule some time off on the weekends so you can enjoy the journey, not just the goal.

Work

You can make a lot of money this year and, if you've been focused on your work for the last couple of years, this is a time when money should flow to you. The Chinese believe the number 8 is indeed the money number and can bring you the fruits of your hard labour.

Because you're cautious and resourceful you'll be able to save more this year, but try not to be too stingy with your money.

Under an 8 year you'll take on new responsibilities. You mustn't do this for the sake of looking good. If you truly like the work that is being offered, by all means take it. But if it's simply for the sake of ego, you'll be very disappointed.

Improving your luck

This year you could be a little reluctant to try new things. But if you are overly cautious, you may miss opportunities. Don't act impulsively on what is being offered, of course, but do be open to trying some alternative things as well.

Be gentle and kind to yourself. By pampering yourself you send out a strong signal to the universe that you are deserving of some rewards.

The 1st, 8th, 15th and 20th hours of Saturdays are the best times for you in 2011.

The numbers 1, 8, 17, 26 and 35 are your lucky numbers.

9 is the year of Mars

Overview

The year 2011 is the final year of a nine-year cycle and this will be dominated by Aries and Mars. You'll be rushing madly to complete many things, so be careful not to overstep the mark of your capability. Work hard but balance your life with adequate rest.

In your relationships you will realise that you are at odds with your partner and want different things. This is the time to talk it out. If the communication between you isn't flowing well, you might find yourself leaving the relationship and moving on to bigger or better things. Worthwhile communication is a two-way street that will benefit both of you.

Love and pleasure

Mars is very pushy and infuses the number 9 with this kind of energy. The upshot is you need to be gentle in conveying your ideas and offering your views. Avoid arguments if you want to improve your relationships.

If you feel it's time for a change, discuss it with your partner. You can work through this feeling together and create an exciting new pathway for your love life. Don't get too angry with the little things in life. Get out and play some sport if you feel you are inappropriately taking out your bad moods on the ones you love.

Work

You have an intense drive and strong capability to achieve anything you choose in 2011. But be careful you don't overdo things, because you are prone to pushing yourself too far. Pace your deadlines, stagger the workload and, if possible, delegate some of the more menial tasks to others so you'll have time to do your own work properly.

Number 9 has an element of leadership associated with it, so you may be asked to take over and lead the group. This brings with it added responsibility but can also inspire you greatly.

Improving your luck

Restlessness is one of the problems that the number 9 brings with it, so you must learn to meditate and pacify your mind so you can take advantage of what the universe has to offer. If you're scattered in your energies, your attention will miss vital opportunities and your relationships could also become rather problematic as well.

Your health and vitality will remain strong as long as you rest adequately and find suitable outlets for your tension.

The 1st, 8th, 15th and 20th hours of Tuesdays will be lucky for you throughout 2011. Your lucky numbers are 9, 18, 27 and 36.

GEMINI

2011:
Your Daily Planner

It's not what you look at that matters; it's what you see

—Henry David Thoreau

There is a little-known branch of astrology called electional astrology, and it can help you select the most appropriate times for many of your day-to-day activities.

Ancient astrologers understood the planetary patterns and how they impacted on each of us. This allowed them to suggest the best possible times to start various important activities. Many farmers today still use this approach: they understand the phases of the Moon, and attest to the fact that planting seeds on certain lunar days produces a far better crop than planting on other days.

The following section covers many areas of day-to-day life, and uses the cycles of the Moon and the combined strength of the other planets to work out the best times to start different types of activity.

So to create your own personal almanac, first select the activity you are interested in, then quickly scan the year for the best months to start it. When you have selected the month, you can finetune your timing by finding the best specific dates. You can then be sure that the planetary energies will be in sync with you, offering you the best possible outcome.

Coupled with what you know about your monthly and weekly trends, the daily planner can be a powerful tool to help you capitalise on opportunities that come your way this year.

Good luck, and may the planets bless you with great success, fortune and happiness in 2011!

Starting Activities

How many times have you made a new year's resolution to begin a diet or be a better person in your relationships? And how many times has it not worked out? Well, part of the reason may be that you started out at the wrong time, because how successful you are is strongly influenced by the position of the Moon and the planets when you begin a particular activity. You will be more successful with the following endeavours if you start them on the days indicated.

Relationships

We all feel more empowered on some days than on others. This is because the planets have some power over us—their movement and their relationships to each other determine the ebb and flow of our energies. And our level of self-confidence and our sense of romantic magnetism play an important part in the way we behave in relationships.

Your daily planner tells you the ideal dates for meeting new friends, initiating a love affair, spending time with family and loved ones—it even tells you the most appropriate times for sexual encounters.

You'll be surprised at how much more impact you can make in your relationships when you tune yourself in to the planetary energies on these special dates.

Falling in love or restoring love

During these times you could expect favourable energies to be present to meet your soulmate. Or, if you've had difficulty in a relationship, you can approach the one you love to rekindle both your and their emotional responses.

January	8, 9, 10, 13, 14, 15, 18, 19, 20, 21
February	4, 5, 6, 9, 10, 11, 14
March	1, 9, 10, 14, 15, 16, 17
April	5, 6, 17, 25, 26
May	3, 4, 6, 7, 8, 9, 10, 11, 14, 15, 22, 23, 24
June	1, 11, 18, 19, 20, 28, 29, 30
July	7, 8, 26, 27, 30, 31
August	3, 12, 13, 14, 22, 23, 27, 31
September	1, 18, 19, 20, 26, 27, 28, 29, 30
October	12, 13, 17, 18, 25, 26, 29, 30, 31
November	2, 3, 4, 5, 6, 9, 17, 29
December	3, 7, 8, 11, 14, 15, 18, 19, 29, 30

Special times with friends and family

Socialising, partying and having a good time with those you enjoy being with is highly favourable under the following dates. These are also excellent days to spend time with family and loved ones in a domestic environment:

January	17, 20, 21
February	2, 9, 10, 11, 18, 19, 20, 21, 22, 23, 24, 28
March	1, 11, 14, 16, 17, 20
April	2, 11, 12, 21, 22, 26
May	6, 9, 10, 11, 14, 15, 22, 23, 24
June	4, 8, 10, 12, 19, 20, 25, 26, 28
July	7, 8, 16, 23, 30, 31
August	4, 5, 6, 7, 13, 20, 27, 31
September	1, 6, 18, 19, 20, 29, 30
October	1, 16, 17, 25, 26
November	2, 12, 13, 17, 26, 29
December	11, 14, 15, 18, 19, 27, 28

Healing or resuming a relationship

If you're trying to get back together with the one you love and need a heart-to-heart or deep and meaningful conversation, you can try the following dates to do so:

January	2, 3, 4, 5, 6, 7, 8, 9, 10, 11, 12, 13, 14, 15, 16, 17, 18, 19, 20, 21, 28
February	1, 2, 4, 5, 6, 7, 21, 22, 23, 24, 28

March	1, 8, 9, 10, 11, 14, 16, 17, 18, 19, 20
April	2, 11, 12, 26
May	1, 6, 7, 8, 9, 10, 11, 12, 13, 15, 19, 22, 24, 25, 26, 27, 28
June	5, 12, 14, 15, 16, 19, 23, 25, 26, 27, 28, 29, 30
July	4, 6, 7, 8, 9, 10, 16, 19, 21, 23, 28, 29, 30, 31
August	1, 2, 3, 13, 15, 16, 20, 27, 29, 30, 31
September	1, 2, 3, 4, 5, 6, 13, 15, 16, 17, 18, 19, 20, 21, 22, 23, 25, 28, 29
October	12, 13, 15, 16, 17, 18, 25, 27, 29
November	2, 4, 5, 6, 15, 16, 17, 26, 29
December	11, 19, 20, 21, 22, 23

Sexual encounters

Physical and sexual energies are well favoured on the following dates. The energies of the planets enhance your moments of intimacy during these times:

January	2, 3, 4, 5, 6, 7, 8, 9, 10, 11, 12, 20, 21, 25
February	7, 8, 18, 19, 20, 21
March	1, 8, 11, 14, 20, 21
April	4, 11, 12, 25, 26, 27, 28, 29
May	2, 9, 10, 11, 14, 15, 22, 23, 24

June	1, 11, 12, 18, 19, 20, 28, 29, 30
July	7, 8, 16, 19, 20, 21, 23, 30
August	3, 12, 13, 14, 20, 22, 27, 31
September	1, 18, 19, 20, 29, 30
October	1, 13, 15, 18, 19, 20, 21, 22, 25, 26
November	2, 3, 11, 15, 16, 17, 18, 21, 22
December	5, 6, 12, 13, 14, 15, 18, 19

Health and wellbeing

Your aura and life force are susceptible to the movements of the planets; in particular, they respond to the phases of the Moon.

The following dates are the most appropriate times to begin a diet, have cosmetic surgery, or seek medical advice. They also tell you when the best times are to help others.

Feeling of wellbeing

Your physical as well as your mental alertness should be strong on these following dates. You can plan your activities and expect a good response from others:

January	7, 9, 10, 11, 12, 13, 14, 18, 20, 21
February	4, 18, 19, 20, 21, 22, 23, 24
March	16, 17, 19, 20
April	2, 7, 12, 20, 22, 25, 26

May	9, 10, 11, 14, 15, 16, 17, 22, 24, 25
June	4, 8, 10, 11, 12, 16, 17, 18, 19, 20, 21, 23, 25, 26
July	7, 8, 9, 10, 26, 27, 30
August	3, 4, 5, 6, 12, 13, 14, 17, 19, 22, 27, 31
September	1, 13, 26, 27, 28, 29, 30
October	1, 16, 17, 25, 26, 30, 31
November	1, 2, 3, 4, 5, 6, 17, 29
December	4, 11, 14, 15, 18, 19, 21, 22, 23, 30

Healing and medical

These times are good for approaching others who have expertise when you need some deeper under-standing. They are also favourable for any sort of healing or medication, and for making appointments with doctors or psychologists. Planning surgery around these dates should bring good results.

Often giving up our time and energy to assist others doesn't necessarily result in the expected outcome. By lending a helping hand to a friend on the following dates, the results should be favour-able:

January	1, 2, 3, 4, 5, 6, 7, 8, 14, 15, 16, 17, 18, 19, 20, 21, 22, 23, 24, 25, 26, 27, 28, 29, 31
February	3, 4, 5, 6, 7, 8, 9, 10, 13, 15, 16, 17, 18, 19, 21, 22, 23, 24, 25, 26, 27

March	4, 9, 10, 11, 12, 15, 16
April	2, 9, 10, 11, 12, 13, 14, 15, 16, 17, 18, 19, 20, 21, 22, 23, 24, 25, 26, 27, 28, 29, 30
May	1, 2, 3, 4, 5, 6, 8, 9, 10, 11, 12, 13, 14, 15, 16, 17, 18, 19, 20, 21, 22, 23, 24, 25, 30
June	23, 26, 28
July	3, 10, 11, 12
August	7, 8, 9, 10, 11, 12, 13, 14, 15, 16, 20, 21, 25
September	23, 25, 26, 27
October	20, 21, 22, 23, 24, 25, 26, 27, 28, 29, 30, 31
November	1, 2, 3, 4, 5, 6, 7, 8, 9, 10, 11, 12, 13, 14, 15, 16, 17, 18, 19, 20, 21, 22, 23, 24, 25, 30
December	1, 2, 3, 4, 5, 6, 7, 8, 9, 10, 30

Money

Money is an important part of life, and involves lots of decisions—decisions about borrowing, investing, spending. The ideal times for transactions are very much influenced by the planets, and whether your investment or nest egg grows or doesn't grow can often be linked to timing. Making your decisions on the following dates could give you a whole new perspective on your financial future.

Managing wealth and money

To build your nest egg it's a good time to open a bank account and invest money on the following dates:

January	2, 3, 9, 10, 11, 12, 13, 14, 15, 16, 17, 18, 19, 20, 21, 22, 24, 28
February	3, 4, 5, 6, 7, 8, 9, 11, 13, 14, 16, 18, 19, 20, 21, 22, 23, 24, 25, 26, 27
March	4, 8, 11, 12, 13, 14, 16, 17, 18, 19
April	2, 7, 8, 9, 10, 11, 12, 13, 16, 17, 18, 19, 20, 21, 22, 23, 24, 25
May	1, 6, 7, 8, 9, 10, 11, 12, 13, 14, 15, 16, 17, 18, 19, 20, 21, 22, 23, 24, 25, 30
June	3, 4, 5, 8, 16, 17, 18, 19, 20, 23, 25, 26, 27, 28
July	4, 5, 6, 7, 8, 9, 10, 11, 12, 16, 23, 25, 28, 29, 30, 31
August	1, 2, 3, 4, 5, 6, 7, 8, 9, 10, 11, 12, 13, 14, 15, 16, 17, 19, 20, 30, 31
September	2, 11, 13, 15, 23, 25, 26, 27, 28, 29, 30
October	1, 2, 3, 4, 5, 6, 7, 8, 13, 14, 15, 16, 17, 18, 19, 21, 24, 25, 26, 27, 28, 29, 30, 31
November	2, 3, 4, 5, 6, 7, 9, 11, 12, 13, 14, 15, 16, 17, 18, 19, 20, 23, 25, 29
December	6, 13, 19, 26, 31

Spending

It's always fun to spend, but the following dates are more in tune with this activity and are likely to give you better results:

January	8, 9, 10, 11, 12, 13, 14, 15
February	9, 11, 18, 19
March	9
April	22
May	6, 7, 8, 9, 10, 11, 12, 13, 14, 17, 18, 19, 20, 21, 22, 23, 24
June	4, 8, 10, 11, 12, 14, 16, 17, 19
July	6, 7, 8, 9, 10, 11, 31
August	1, 2, 3, 4, 5, 6, 15, 16, 17, 18, 19, 30, 31
September	1, 2, 3, 4, 17, 19, 28, 29, 30
October	12, 13, 14, 15, 16, 17, 18, 19, 27, 28, 29, 30, 31
November	2, 3, 4, 5, 6, 7
December	3, 4, 5, 22, 23

Selling

If you're thinking of selling something, whether it is small or large, consider the following dates as ideal times to do so:

January	2, 3, 9, 10, 11, 12, 13, 14, 15, 16, 17, 18, 19, 20, 22, 24, 28

February	3, 4, 5, 6, 7, 8, 9, 11, 13, 14, 16, 18, 19, 20, 21, 22, 23, 24, 25, 26, 27
March	4, 8, 11, 12, 13, 14, 16, 17, 18, 19
April	2, 7, 8, 9, 10, 11, 12, 13, 16, 17, 18, 19, 20, 21, 22, 23, 24
May	1, 6, 7, 8, 9, 10, 11, 12, 13, 14, 15, 16, 17, 18, 19, 20, 21, 22, 23, 24, 25, 26, 30
June	3, 4, 5, 8, 16, 17, 18, 19, 20, 23, 25, 26, 27, 28
July	4, 5, 6, 7, 8, 9, 10, 11, 12, 16, 23, 25, 28, 29, 30, 31
August	1, 2, 3, 4, 5, 6, 7, 8, 9, 10, 11, 12, 13, 14, 15, 16, 17, 19, 20, 30, 31
September	2, 11, 13, 15, 23, 25, 26, 27, 28, 29, 30
October	1, 2, 3, 4, 5, 6, 7, 8, 13, 14, 15, 16, 17, 18, 19, 21, 24, 25, 26, 27, 28, 29, 30, 31
November	2, 3, 4, 5, 6, 7, 9, 11, 12, 13, 14, 15, 16, 17, 18, 19, 20, 23, 25, 29
December	2, 3, 4, 5, 6, 7, 11, 30

Borrowing

Few of us like to borrow money, but if you must, taking out a loan on the following dates will be positive:

January	1, 20, 21, 26, 27, 28, 31
February	1, 2, 22, 23, 24
March	1, 22, 23, 26, 27, 29, 31
April	1, 18, 19, 22, 23, 24, 25, 26, 27, 28, 29
May	17, 18, 19, 20, 21, 22, 23, 24, 25, 26
June	16, 17, 18, 19, 22
July	15, 16, 28, 29, 30
August	15, 16, 24, 25, 26, 27, 28
September	21, 22
October	21
November	14, 15, 16, 17, 23, 24
December	12, 13, 14, 15, 20, 21, 22, 23, 24

Speculation and investment

To invest your money and get a good return on that investment, try taking a punt on the following dates:

January	3, 4, 5, 11, 12, 18, 19, 24, 25, 31
February	1, 7, 8, 14, 15, 20, 21, 27, 28
March	6, 7, 8, 14, 15, 20, 21, 26, 27
April	2, 3, 4, 10, 11, 16, 17, 22, 23, 24, 30
May	1, 7, 8, 14, 15, 20, 21, 27, 28, 29
June	3, 4, 5, 10, 11, 16, 17, 23, 24, 25
July	1, 2, 7, 8, 14, 15, 21, 22, 28, 29

August	3, 4, 10, 11, 17, 18, 19, 24, 25, 26, 31
September	1, 6, 7, 13, 14, 15, 21, 22, 27, 28
October	3, 4, 5, 11, 12, 18, 19, 25, 26, 31
November	1, 7, 8, 14, 15, 16, 21, 22, 27, 28
December	4, 5, 6, 12, 13, 18, 19, 25, 26, 31

Work and education

Your career is important to you, and continual improvement of your skills is therefore also crucial, professionally, mentally and socially. These dates will help you find out the most appropriate times to improve your professional talents and commence new work or education associated with your work.

You may need to decide when to start learning a new skill, when to ask for a promotion, and even when to make an important career change. Here are the days when your mental and educational power is strong.

Learning new skills

Educational pursuits are lucky and bring good results on the following dates:

January	16, 17
February	12, 13
March	11, 12, 13, 18, 19
April	7, 8, 9, 14, 15
May	5, 6, 12, 13

June	2, 8, 9, 14, 15
July	5, 6, 11, 12, 13
August	1, 2, 8, 9, 29, 30
September	4, 5
October	1, 2, 29, 30
November	25, 26
December	9, 10

Changing career path or profession

If you're feeling stuck and need to move into a new professional activity, changing jobs is recommended at these times:

January	4, 5, 13, 14, 15
February	9, 10, 11
March	1, 2, 3, 9, 10, 11, 12, 18, 19, 20, 21
April	5, 6, 7, 8, 9, 14, 15, 16, 17, 25, 26
May	3, 4, 12, 13, 22, 23, 24
June	1, 2, 8, 9, 18, 19, 20, 28, 29, 30
July	5, 6, 14, 26, 27
August	3, 4, 10, 11, 22, 23, 29, 30, 31
September	1, 6, 7, 8, 9, 10, 18, 19, 20, 27, 28
October	3, 4, 5, 16, 17, 25, 26, 31
November	1, 2, 3, 9, 10, 29, 30
December	1, 7, 8, 9, 10, 11, 18, 19, 25, 26, 27, 28

Promotion, professional focus and hard work

To increase your mental focus and achieve good results from the work you do; promotions are also likely on the dates that follow:

January	3, 9, 10, 11, 12, 13, 14, 18
February	22, 23, 24, 25, 26, 27, 28
March	8, 10, 11, 13, 14, 16, 17, 18, 19
April	11, 12
May	6, 7, 8, 9, 10, 11, 12, 13, 15, 16, 17, 19, 21, 22, 23, 24
June	4, 5, 8, 11, 12, 14, 15, 16, 17, 19
July	16, 18, 19, 20, 23, 24, 25, 28, 29, 30
August	1, 2, 14, 15, 16, 17, 19, 30
September	1, 2, 3, 4, 5, 6, 11, 13, 16, 17, 19
October	13, 15, 16, 17, 18, 19
November	2, 4, 5, 6, 7, 12
December	25, 26

Travel

Setting out on a holiday or adventurous journey is exciting. Here are the most favourable times for doing this. Travel on the following dates is likely to give you a sense of fulfilment:

January	9, 10, 11, 12, 16, 17, 18, 19
February	4, 5, 6, 7, 15

March	19
April	7, 8, 9, 10, 11
May	15
June	4, 8, 10, 11
July	1, 5, 6
August	1, 2, 3, 4, 8
September	27, 28
October	1, 3, 4, 29, 30, 31
November	1, 4, 5, 6
December	3, 4, 5, 25, 29, 30

Beauty and grooming

Believe it or not, cutting your hair or nails has a powerful effect on your body's electromagnetic energy. If you cut your hair or nails at the wrong time of the month, you can reduce your level of vitality significantly. Use these dates to ensure you optimise your energy levels by staying in tune with the stars:

Haircuts

January	1, 2, 8, 9, 10, 16, 17, 28, 29, 30
February	25, 26
March	4, 5, 11, 12, 13, 14, 25, 31
April	1, 7, 8, 9, 20, 21, 27, 28, 29
May	5, 6, 18, 19, 25, 26

June	1, 2, 14, 15, 21, 22, 28, 29, 30
July	11, 12, 13, 18, 19, 20, 26, 27
August	8, 9, 15, 16, 22, 23
September	4, 5, 11, 12, 18, 19, 20
October	1, 2, 8, 9, 10, 16, 17, 29, 30
November	4, 5, 6, 12, 13, 25, 26
December	2, 3, 9, 10, 11, 23, 24, 29, 30

Cutting nails

January	11, 12, 13, 14, 15, 18, 19, 20, 21
February	7, 8, 9, 10, 11, 14, 16
March	6, 8, 9, 10, 14, 15
April	2, 3, 5, 6
May	4, 7, 8, 9, 10, 11, 27, 28, 29, 30, 31
June	3, 4, 5, 6, 7, 23, 25, 26, 27
July	1, 2, 3, 21, 22, 23, 24, 25, 28, 29, 30, 31
August	17, 19, 20, 24, 25, 26
September	13, 16, 17, 21, 22, 23, 24
October	11, 13, 15, 18, 19, 20, 21, 22
November	15, 16, 17, 18
December	4, 5, 6, 7, 8

Therapies, massage and self-pampering

January	1, 2, 8, 9, 10, 16, 17, 28, 29, 30
February	5, 6, 12, 13, 25, 26
March	4, 5, 11, 12, 13, 24, 25, 31
April	1, 7, 8, 9, 20, 21, 27, 28, 29
May	5, 6, 18, 19, 25, 26
June	1, 2, 14, 15, 21, 22, 28, 29, 30
July	11, 12, 13, 18, 19, 20, 26, 27
August	8, 9, 15, 16, 22, 23
September	4, 5, 11, 12, 18, 19, 20
October	1, 2, 8, 9, 10, 16, 17, 29, 30
November	4, 5, 6, 12, 13, 25, 26
December	2, 3, 9, 10, 11, 23, 24, 29, 30